I0201304

TURKEY:

A Past and A Future

TURKEY:

A Past and A Future

A. J. TOYNBEE

serenity
Publishers, LLC
ROCKVILLE, MARYLAND
2009

Turkey: A Past and A Future by A. J. Toynbee in its current format, copyright © Serenity Publishers 2009. This book, in whole or in part, may not be copied or reproduced in its current format by any means, electronic, mechanical or otherwise without the permission of the publisher.

The original text has been reformatted for clarity and to fit this edition.

Serenity Publishers & associated logos are trademarks or registered trademarks of Serenity Publishers, Rockville, Maryland. All other trademarks are properties of their respective owners.

This book is presented as is, without any warranties (implied or otherwise) as to the accuracy of the production, text or translation. The publisher does not take responsibility for any typesetting, formatting, translation or other errors which may have occurred during the production of this book.

ISBN: 978-1-60450-705-8

Published by Serenity Publishers
An Arc Manor Company
P. O. Box 10339
Rockville, MD 20849-0339
www.SerenityPublishers.com

Printed in the United States of America/United Kingdom

CONTENTS

ço

I

THE PAST

What is Turkey? It is a name which explains nothing, for no formula can embrace the variety of the countries marked "Ottoman" on the map: the High Yemen, with its monsoons and tropical cultivation; the tilted rim of the Hedjaz, one desert in a desert zone that stretches from the Sahara to Mongolia; the Mesopotamian rivers, breaking the desert with a strip of green; the pine-covered mountain terraces of Kurdistan, which gird in Mesopotamia as the hills of the North-West Frontier of India gird the Plains; the Armenian highlands, bleak as the Pamirs, which feed Mesopotamia with their snows and send it the soil they cannot keep themselves; the Anatolian peninsula—an offshoot of Central Europe with its rocks and fine timber and mountain streams, but nursing a steppe in its heart more intractable than the Puszta of Hungary; the coast-lands—Trebizond and Ismid and Smyrna clinging to the Anatolian mainland and Syria interposing itself between the desert and the sea, but all, with their vines and olives and sharp contours, keeping true to the Mediterranean; and then the waterway of narrows and land-locked sea and narrows again which links the Mediterranean with the Black Sea and the Russian hinterland, and which has not its like in the world.

The cities of Turkey are as various as the climes, with the added impress of many generations of men: Adrianople, set at a junction of rivers within the circle of the Thracian downs, a fortress since its foundation, well chosen for the tombs of the Ottoman conquerors; Constantinople, capital of empires where races meet but never mix, mistress of trade routes vital to the existence of vast regions beyond her horizon—Central Europe trafficking south-eastward overland and Russia south-westward by sea; Smyrna, the port by which men go up and down between Anatolia and the Aegean, the foothold on the Asiatic mainland which the Greeks have never lost; Konia, between the mountain girdle and the central steppe, where native Anatolia has always stood at bay, guarding her race and religion against the influences of the coasts; Aleppo, where, if Turkey were a unity, the centre of Turkey would be found, the city where, if anywhere, the races of the Near East have mingled—building their courses into her fortress walls from the polygonal work of the Hittite founders to the battlements that kept out the Crusaders—and now the half-way point of a railway surveyed along an immemorially ancient route, but unfinished like the history of Aleppo herself; Van by its upland lake, overhanging the Mesopotamian lowlands and with the writing of their culture graven on its cliffs, yet living a life apart like some Swiss canton and half belonging to the infinite north; Bagdad, the incarnation for the last millennium of an eternal city that shifts its site as its rivers shift their beds—from Seleucia to Bagdad, from Babylon to Seleucia, from Kish to Babylon—but which always springs up again, like Delhi, within a few parasangs of its last ruins, in an area that is an irresistible focus of population; Basra amid its palm-groves, so far down stream that it belongs to the Indian Ocean—the port from which Sinbad set sail for fairyland, and from which less mythical Arab seamen spread their religion and civilisation far over African coasts and Malayan Indies; these, and besides them almost all the holy cities of mankind: Kerbela, between the Euphrates and the desert, where, under Sunni rule, the Shias of Persia and India have still visited the tombs of their saints and buried their dead; Jerusalem, where Jew and Christian, Orthodox, Catholic and Protestant, Armenian and Abyssinian, have their common shrines and separate quarters; Mekka and Medina in the heart of the desert, beyond which their fame would never have passed but for a well and a mart and a precinct of idols and the Prophet who overthrew them; and there are the cities on the Pilgrim Road (linked now by railway with Medina, the nearer of the *Haramein):* Beirut the port, with its electric trams and newspapers, the Smyrna of the Arab lands; and Damascus the oasis, looking out over the desert instead of the sea, and harbour not of ships but of camel-caravans.

The names of these cities call up, like an incantation, the memory of the civilisations which grew in them to greatness and sank in them to decay: Mesopotamia, a great heart of civilisation which is cold to-day, but which beat so strongly for five thousand years that its pulses were felt from Siberia to the Pillars of Hercules and influenced the taste and technique of the Scandinavian bronze age; the Assyrians, who extended the political marches of Mesopotamia towards the north, and turned them into a military monarchy that devastated the motherland and all other lands and peoples from the Tigris to the sea; the Hebrews, discovering a world-religion in their hill-country overlooking the coast; the Sabaeans, whose queen made the first pilgrimage to Jerusalem, coming from Yemen across the Hedjaz when Mekka and Medina were still of no account; the Philistines and Phoenicians of the Syrian sea-board, who were discovering the Atlantic and were too busy to listen to the Hebrew prophets in their hinterland; the Ionians, who opened up the Black Sea and created a poetry, philosophy, science, and architecture which are still the life-blood of ours, before they were overwhelmed, like the Phoenicians before them, by a continental military power; the Hittites, who first transmitted the fruitful influences of Mesopotamia to the Ionian coasts—a people as mysterious to their contemporaries as to ourselves, maturing unknown in the fastnesses of Anatolia, raising up a sudden empire that raided Mesopotamia and colonised the Syrian valleys, and then succumbing to waves of northern invasion. All these people rose and fell within the boundaries of Turkey, held the stage of the world for a time, and left their mark on its history. There is a romance about their names, a wonderful variety and intensity in their vanished life; yet they are not more diverse than their modern successors, in whose veins flows their blood and whose possibilities are only dwarfed by their achievements.

There were less than twenty million people in Turkey before the War, and during it the Government has caused a million or so to perish by massacre, starvation, or disease. Yet, in spite of this daemoniac effort after uniformity, they are still the strangest congeries of racial and social types that has ever been placed at a single Government's mercy. The Ottoman Empire is named after the Osmanli, but you might search long before you found one among its inhabitants. These Osmanlis are a governing class, indigenous only in Constantinople and a few neighbouring towns, but planted here and there, as officers and officials, over the Ottoman territories. They come of a clan of Turkish nomads, recruited since the thirteenth century by converts, forced or voluntary, from most of Christendom, and crossed with the blood of slave-women from all the world. They are hardly a race. Tradition fortified by inertia makes them what they are, and also their Turkish language, which serves them for business of state and for a literature, though not without an infusion of Persian and Arabic idioms said to amount to 95 per cent. of the vocabulary.[1]

This artificial language is hardly a link between Osmanli officialdom and the Turkish peasantry of Anatolia, which speaks Turkish dialects derived from tribes that drifted in, some as late as the Osmanlis, some two centuries before. Nor has this Turkish-speaking peasantry much in common with the Turkish nomads who still wander over the central Anatolian steppe and have kept their blood pure; for the peasantry has reverted physically to the native stock, which held Anatolia from time immemorial and absorbs all newcomers that mingle with it on its soil. Thus there are three distinct "Turkish" elements in Turkey, divided by blood and vocation and social type; and even if we reckon all who speak some form of Turkish as one group, they only amount to 30 or 40 per cent. of the whole population of the Empire.

The rest are alien to the Turks and to one another. Those who speak Arabic are as strong numerically as the Turks, or stronger, but they too are divided, and their unity is a problem of the future. There are pure-bred Arab nomads of the desert; there are Arabs who have settled in towns or on the land, some within the

---

1   Tekin Alp: "The Turkish and Pan-Turkish Ideal" (Weimar: Gustav Kiepenheuer, 1915). The percentage is of course an exaggeration.

last generation, like the Muntefik in Mesopotamia, some a millennium or two ago, like the Meccan Koreish, but who still retain their tribal consciousness of race; there are Arabs in name who have nothing Arabic about them but their language—most of the peasantry of Syria are such, and the inhabitants of ancient centres of population like Damascus or Bagdad; in Syria many of these "Arabs" are Christians, and some Christians, though they speak Arabic, have retained their separate sense of nationality—notably the Roman Catholic Maronites of the Lebanon—and would hardly be considered as Arabs either by themselves or by their neighbours. The same is true of the Druses, another remnant of an earlier stock, which has preserved its identity under the guise of Islam so heretically conceived as to rank as an independent religion. As for the Yemenis—they will resent the imputation, for no Arabs count up their genealogies so zealously as they, but there is more East African than Semitic blood in their veins. They are men of the moist, fertile tropics, brown of skin, and working half naked in their fields, like the peoples of Southern India and Bengal. And on the opposite fringes of the Arabic-speaking area there are fragments of population whose language is Semitic but pre-Arabic[2]—the Jacobite Christians of the Tor-Abdin, and the Nestorians of the Upper Zab, who once, under the Caliphs, were the industrious Christian peasantry of Mesopotamia, but now are shepherds and hillmen among the Kurds. The Kurds themselves are more scattered than any other stock in Turkey, and divided tribe against tribe, but taken together they rank third in numerical strength, after the Arabs and Turks. There are mountain Kurds and Kurds of the plain, hus-

---

2   In the sense of having preceded Arabic in this region, for in itself, and in its original area, Arabic is as old a language an any other variety of Semitic.

bandmen and herdsmen, Kurds who have kept to their original homes along the eastern frontier, and Kurds who, under Ottoman auspices, have spread themselves over the Armenian plateau, the North Mesopotamian steppes, the Taurus valleys, and the hinterland of the Black Sea.

The chief thing the Kurds have in common is the Persian dialect they speak, but it is usual to class as Kurds any and every community in the Kurdish area which is not Turkish or Arab and can by courtesy be called Moslem (the Kurds, for that matter, are only Moslems skin-deep). Such communities abound: the Dersim highlands, in particular, are an ethnographical museum; "Kizil-Bashi" is a general name for their kind; only the Yezidis, though they speak good Kurdish, are distinguished from the rest for their idiosyncrasy of worshipping Satan under the form of a peacock (Allah, they argue, is good-natured and does not need to be propitiated) and they are repudiated with one accord by Moslem and Christian.

But not all the scattered elements in Turkey are isolated or primitive. The Greeks and Armenians, for instance, are, or were, the most energetic, intellectual, liberal elements in Turkey, the natural intermediaries between the other races and western civilisation—"were" rather than "are," because the Ottoman Government has taken ruthless steps to eliminate just these two most valuable elements among its subjects. The urban Greeks survive in centres like Smyrna and Constantinople, but the Greek peasantry of Thrace and Anatolia has mostly been driven over the frontier since the Second Balkan War. As for the Armenians, the Government has been destroying them by massacre and deportation since April, 1915—business and professional men, peasants and shepherds, women and children—without discrimination or pity. A third of the Ottoman Armenians may still survive; a tenth of them are safe within the Russian and British lines. Fortunately half this nation, and the majority of the Greeks, live outside the Ottoman frontiers, and are beyond the Osmanli's power.

To compensate for its depopulation of the countries under its dominion, the Ottoman Government, during the last fifty years, has been settling them with Moslem immigrants from its own lost provinces or from other Moslem lands that have changed their rulers. These "Mouhadjirs" are reckoned, from first to last, at three-quarters of a million, drawn from the most diverse stocks—Bosniaks and Pomaks and Albanians, Algerines and Tripolitans, Tchetchens and Circassians. Numbers have been planted recently on the lands of dispossessed Armenians and Greeks. They add many more elements to the confusion of tongues, but they are probably destined to be absorbed or to die out. The Circassians, in particular, who are the most industrious (though most unruly) and preserve their nationality best, also succumb most easily to transplantation, through refusal to adapt their Caucasian clothes and habits to Anatolian or Mesopotamian conditions of life.

All this is Turkey, and we come back to our original question: What common factor accounts for the name? What has stained this coat of many colours to one political hue? The answer is simple: Blood. Turkey, the Ottoman state, is not a unity, climatic, geographical, racial, or economic; it is a pretension, enforced by bloodshed and violence whenever and wherever the Osmanli Government has power.

It is a complex pretension. The first impulse, and the traditional method by which it has been given effect, came from a little tribe of pagan, nomadic Turks who wandered into Anatolia from Central Asia in the thirteenth century A.D. and were granted camping grounds by the reigning Turkish Sultan of the country—for Anatolia was already Turkish two centuries before the Osmanlis appeared on the scene. But to call them Osmanlis is to anticipate the next stage in their history. They are named after Osman, their first leader's son, and he after the third successor of the Prophet—it was a good Moslem name, and he took it when he was converted to Islam and organised his pagan tent-dwellers into a settled Mohammedan State in the north-western hills of Anatolia, on the borders of Christendom. A tribe had become a march, and the final stage was from march to empire.

From this point onwards Ottoman history singularly resembles the history of the Osmanlis' present allies. The March of Brandenburg, the March of Austria, and the March of Osman—they were each founded as the outer bulwarks of a civilisation, and all erected themselves into centres of military ascendancy over their fellow-countrymen and co-religionists to the rear as well as the strangers opposite their front. The Osmanlis may have been more savage in their methods than the marchmen of Germany—though hardly, perhaps, than the Teutonic Knights who prepared the soil of Prussia for the Hohenzollerns. The Teutonic Knights exterminated their victims; the Osmanlis drained theirs of their blood by taking a tribute of their male children, educating them as Moslems, and training them as recruits for an Ottoman standing army. Their first expansion was forwards into Christian Europe; their capital shifted from a village in the hills to the city of Brusa on the Asiatic shore of Marmora, from Brusa across the Dardanelles to Adrianople, from Adrianople to the imperial city on the Bosphorus; and, with the capture of Constantinople, the Osmanli Sultans usurped the pretensions of East Rome, as the Hapsburgs and Hohenzollerns the emblems of Charlemagne and Caesar Augustus.

Byzantium has become a very potent element in the Osmanlis' character, more potent than the habits of the march or the instinct of the steppes. It has dictated their system of administration, dominated their outlook on life, penetrated their blood. But the heritage of "Rum" is not the final factor in the Ottoman Empire as it exists to-day; for after the successors of Osman had founded their military monarchy with blood and iron on the ruins of one-third of Europe, they turned eastwards, with a genuinely Oriental gesture, and overran kingdoms and lands with the apparently mechanical impetus of all Asiatic conquerors, from Sargon of Akkad and Cyrus the Persian to Jenghis Khan and Timur. The stoutest opponent of the Osmanlis in Asia was the Anatolian Sultanate of Karaman—Moslem, Turkish, and the legitimate heir of those Seljuk Turkish Sultans who had given Osman's father his first footing in the land. Osmanli and Karamanli fought on equal terms, but when Karaman was overthrown there was no power left in Asia that could stop the Osmanlis' advance. The Egyptians and Persians had no more chance against Ottoman discipline and artillery than the last Darius had against the Macedonians. A campaign or two brought Sultan Selim the First from the Taurus to Cairo; a few more campaigns at intervals during the sixteenth and seventeenth centuries, when Ottoman armies could be spared from Europe, drove the Persians successively out of Armenia and Mosul and Bagdad. And thus, by accident, as it were, in the pursuit of more coveted things, the Osmanlis acquired "Turkey-in-Asia," which is all that remains to them now and all that concerns us here.

"Turkey-in-Asia" is a transitory phenomenon, a sort of chrysalis which enshrouded the countries of Western Asia because they were exhausted and needed torpor as a preliminary to recuperation. Many calamities had fallen upon them during the five centuries before the chrysalis formed. The break-up of the Arab Caliphate of Bagdad had led to an interminable, meaningless conflict among a host of petty Moslem States; the wearing struggle between Islam and Christendom had been intensified by the Crusades; and waves of nomadic invaders, each more destructive and more irresistible than the last, had swept over Moslem Asia out of the steppes and deserts of the north-east. The most terrible were the Mongols, who sacked Bagdad in 1258, and gave the *coup de grace* to the civilisation of Mesopotamia. And then, when the native productiveness of the Near East was ruined, the transit trade between Europe and the Indies, which had belonged to it from the earliest times and had been the second source of its prosperity, was taken from it by the western seafarers who discovered the ocean routes. The pall of Ottoman dominion only descended when life was extinct.

The Osmanlis, whose nomadic forefathers had fled before the face of the Mongols out of Central Asia, took the heritage which had slipped from the Mongols' grasp, and gathered all threads of authority in Western Asia into their hands. The most valuable spoil of their Asiatic conquests was the Caliphate. Hulaku, the sacker of Bagdad, had put the Caliph Mustasim to death, and the remnant of the Abbasids had kept up a shadowy succession at Cairo, under the protection of the Sultan of Egypt. Selim the Osmanli, when he entered Cairo as a conqueror in 1517, caused the contemporary Abbasid to cede his title, for what it was worth, to him and his successors. It was a doubtful title, scorned by all Shias and regarded coldly by many Sunni rulers who were unwilling to recognise a spiritual superior in their most formidable temporal rival. But such as it was, it strengthened the Osmanli's hold on his dominions. Caliph of Islam, victorious guardian of the Moslem marches, and heir by conquest of imperial Rum, the Osmanli Sultan held his Asiatic provinces with ease; but the best security for his tenure was the misery to which they were reduced. Commerce and cultivation ebbed, population dwindled, and nomads still drifted in upon what once had been settled lands. The Ottoman Government, desiring a barrier against Persia, encouraged the Kurds to spread themselves over Armenia; it welcomed less the Shammar and Anazeh Arabs, who broke over the Euphrates about the year 1700 and turned the last fields of Northern Mesopotamia to desolation; but it was too impotent or indifferent to turn them out. Western Asia lay fallow under the Ottoman cannon-wheels. There have been fallow periods before in the slow rhythm of its life—under the Persians, for instance, who overran all lands and peoples of the East in the sixth century B.C., overshadowed the Greeks for a moment, as the Osmanlis overshadowed Europe, halted, too massive for offence but seemingly unassailable, and then collapsed pitifully before the probing spears of Alexander.

The Osmanlis are passing at this moment as the Achaemenids passed then. They lost the last of Europe in the Balkan War, and with it their prestige as increasers of Islam; the growth of national consciousness among their subjects, not least among the Turks themselves, has loosened the foundations of their military empire, as of the other military empires with which they are allied. They forfeited the Caliphate when they proclaimed the Holy War against the Allied Powers—inciting Moslems to join one Christian coalition against another, not in defence of their religion, but for Ottoman political aggrandisement. They lost it morally when this incitement was left unheeded by the Moslem world; they lost it in deed when the Sherif of Mekka asserted his rights as the legitimate guardian of the Holy Cities, drove out the Ottoman garrison from Mekka, and allied himself with the other independent princes of Arabia. All the props of Ottoman dominion in Asia have fallen away, but nothing dooms it so surely as the breath of life that is stirring over the dormant lands and peoples once more. The cutting of the Suez Canal has led the highways of commerce back to the Nearer East; the democracy and nationalism of Europe have been extending their influence over Asiatic races. On whatever terms the War is concluded, one far-reaching result is certain already: there will be a political and economic revival in Western Asia, and the direction of this will not be in Ottoman hands.

We are thus witnessing the foundation of a new era as momentous, if not as dramatic, as Alexander's passage of the Dardanelles. The Ottoman vesture has waxed old, and something can be discerned of the new forms that are emerging from beneath it; their outstanding features are worth our attention.

II

THE PRESENT

The new Turkish Nationalism is the immediate factor to be reckoned with. It is very new—newer than the Young Turks, and sharply opposed to the original Young Turkish programme—but it has established its ascendancy. It decided Turkey's entry into the War, and is the key to the current policy of the Ottoman Government.

The Young Turks were not Nationalists from the beginning; the "Committee of Union and Progress" was founded in good faith to liberate and reconcile all the inhabitants of the Empire on the principles of the French Revolution. At the Committee's congress in 1909 the Nationalists were shouted down with the cry: "Our goal is organisation and nothing else."[3] But Young Turkish ideals rapidly narrowed. Liberalism gave way to Panislamism, Panislamism to Panturanianism, and the "Ottoman State Idea" changed from "Liberty, Equality, and Fraternity" to the Turkification of non-Turkish nationalities by force.

---

3 "The Turkish and Pan-Turkish Ideal," by Tekin Alp.

"The French Ideal," writes the Nationalist Tekin Alp in *Thoughts on the Nature and Plan of a Greater Turkey,* "is in contradiction to the needs and conditions of the age." By contrast, "the Turkish national movement does not exhibit the failings of the earlier movements. It is in every way adapted to the intellectual standard and feelings of the nation. It also keeps pace with the ideas of the age, which have for some decades centred round the principle of Nationality. In adopting Turkish Nationalism as the basis of their national policy, the Turks have only abandoned an abnormal state of affairs and thereby placed themselves on a level with modern nations."[4]

The development of Nationalism among the Turks was a natural phenomenon. Starting in the West, the movement has been spreading for a century through Central Europe, Hungary, and the Balkans, till from the Turks' former subjects it has passed to the Turks themselves. Chance played its part. Dr. Nazim Bey, for instance, the General Secretary of the "Union and Progress" Committee, is said to have been fired by a work of M. Leon Cahun's on the early history of the Turks and Mongols, lent him by the French Consul-General at Salonika, and the movement was, and still is, confined to a small *intelligentsia.* But that is the case with other national movements too, and does not hinder them from being powerful forces. Turkish Nationalism was kept alive after 1909 by a small group of enthusiasts at Salonika—their leader was Ziya Bey, who had come up to the Young Turk Congress from Diarbekir, and was one of the first converts to the new idea. It gained ground suddenly during, the Balkan War. The shock of defeat produced a craving for regeneration; the final loss of Europe turned the minds of the Osmanlis to the pos-

---

4   "The Turkish and Pan-Turkish Ideal," by Tekin Alp.

sibilities of Asia, and they were struck by the action of several prominent Russian subjects of Turco-Tatar nationality, who, out of racial sympathy, had given their services to the Ottoman Government in this time of adversity. As Tekin Alp expresses it:

"The Turks realised that, in order to live, they must become essentially Turkish, become a nation, be themselves.... The Turkish nation turned aside its gaze from the lost territory and looked instead upon Turania, the ideal country of the future."

Two years later this "New Orientation" had so mastered the Ottoman Government that it drew them into the European War.

There are many aims within the new Turkish horizon. Some of them are negative and non-political, some practical and extremely aggressive. Ziya Bey's adherents first took in hand the purification of the Turkish language. A Turkish poet had endeavoured before to dispense with the 95 per cent. (?) of the vocabulary that was borrowed from Persian and Arabic, and "his poetry had to be published in small provincial papers because the important newspapers of the towns would not accept it." The established writers in the traditional style made a hard fight, but Tekin Alp claims that the *Yeni Lisan* (New Language) "is to-day in possession of an absolute and unlimited authority." Borrowed rhythms have been banned as well as borrowed words, and there is even an agitation to replace the Arabic script by a new Turkish alphabet—an imitation of the Albanian movement which was opposed so fiercely by the Turks themselves before the Balkan War. In 1913 the Government stepped in with the foundation of a "Turkish Academy" *(Turk Bilgi Derneyi),* and the Ministry of Education started an "Institute of Terminology," "Conservatoire," and "Writing and Translation Committee." The translation of foreign masterpieces as an incentive to a new national literature was in the programme of Ziya Bey's society, the *Yeni Hayat* (New Life). Their most cherished plan was to translate the Koran and the Friday Sermon, to have the Khutba (Prayer for the Caliph) recited in Turkish, and to remove the Arabic texts from the walls of the mosques;[5] the eyes and ears of Turkish Moslems were to be saved from the contamination of an anti-national language; but the campaign against Arabic passed over into an attack upon Islam.

"The Turkish Nationalists," Tekin Alp explains, "have made great efforts to nationalise religion itself, and to give it the impress of the Turkish national spirit. This idea was zealously supported by a fortnightly periodical, and one of the noblest tasks undertaken by it has been the translation of the Koran into Turkish. This is a reform of the greatest importance. It is well known that the translation of the Koran has hitherto been considered a sin. The Nationalists have cut themselves off from this superstitious prejudice and have had three translations made, the above-mentioned and two others."

On this issue the Nationalists broke a lance with the *Islamjis*, or "clericals," as Tekin Alp prefers to call them.

"Because it is written in the Koran that Islam knows no nationalities, but only Believers, the *Islamjis* thought that to occupy oneself with national questions was to act against the interests and principles of Islam itself.... According to the Nationalists, the pronouncement in the Koran was directed exclusively against the very

---

5   *The Near East,* 30th March, 1917, p. 507; see also Tekin Alp.

frequent dissensions of clans and parties in the various Arab races." (A sneer which is meant to have a modern application.) "Although the Nationalists proclaim themselves the most zealous followers of Mohammed, nevertheless they do not conceal the fact that their interpretation of Islam is not the same as that of the Arabs. They maintain that the Turks cannot interpret the Koran in the same manner as the Arabs.... Their idea of God is also different."

This amazing *Kulturkampf* is quite possibly a reminiscence of Bismarckian Germany, for Turkish Nationalism is saturated with forgotten European moods, and its vein of Romanticism is as antiquated as the Kaiser's. It has taken Attila to its heart, and rehabilitated Jenghis Khan, Timur, Oghuz, and the rest with the erudition of a Turanian Walter Scott.

"My Attila, my Jenghis," sings Ziya Goek Alp, "these heroic figures, which stand for the proud fame of my race, appear on the dry pages of the history books as covered with shame and disgrace, while in reality they are no less than Alexander and Caesar. Still better known to my heart is Oghuz Khan.[6] In me he still lives in all his fame and greatness. Oghuz Khan delights and inspires my heart and causes me to sing psalms of gladness. The fatherland of the Turks is not Turkey or Turkestan, but the broad eternal land of Turania."

The Ministry of *Evkaf* (Religious Endowments) recently made a grant of L50,000 (Turkish) towards the publication of works on these worthies; the students at the Military College in Constantinople are alleged to have been diverted from their studies by their devotion to such literature, and on the eve of the War the Professor of Military Education there is reported to have

---

6   The legendary ancestor of the Turkish race.

delivered the following address to an instruction class of reserve officers:

"We are, gentlemen, before all, Turks. I wonder why we are called Ottomans, for who is Osman after whom we are named? He is a Turk from Altai, who overran this country with his Turkish Army. Therefore it is more of an honour to us to be named after his origin than after himself. We have so far been deceived by the ignorance of our forebears, and fie on these forebears who made us forget our nationality.... Be sure that Turkish nationality is better for us than Islam, and racial pride is one of the greatest social virtues."[7]

These extravagances must not be taken too literally. The Young Turk politicians, though they have embarked on a Nationalist policy, are not so reckless as to break openly with Islam or to denounce the founder of their State. They see clearly enough that Turkish Nationalism carried to a logical extreme is incompatible with the Ottoman pretension, and they favour the view, so severely criticised by Tekin Alp, "that all three groups of ideas—Ottomanism, Islamism, and the Turkish Movement—should work side by side and together." But, with this reservation, they follow the doctrinaires, who on their part are quite ready to press Islam into their service. Tekin Alp candidly admits that

"They sought after a judicious mingling of the religious and national impulses. They realised only too clearly that the still abstract ideals of Nationalism could not be expected to attract the masses, the lower classes, composed of uneducated and illiterate people. It was found more expedient to reach these classes under the flag of religion."

7   *The Near East,* loc. cit.

This sentence reveals in a flash one motive of the Armenian "Deportations," which followed Turkey's intervention in the War; and a celebrated German authority, in a memorial[8] written in 1916, gives this very explanation of their origin.

"Turkey's entry into the War," he writes, "was unwelcome to Turkish society in Constantinople, whose sympathies were with France, as well as to the mass of the people, but the Panislamic propaganda and the military dictatorship were able to stifle all opposition. The proclamation of the 'Holy War' produced a general agitation of the Mohammedan against the Christian elements in the Empire, and the Christian nationalities had soon good reason to fear that Turkish chauvinism would make use of Mohammedan fanaticism to make the War popular with the mass of the Mohammedan population."

The evidence presented in the British Blue Book on the *Treatment of Armenians in the Ottoman Empire*[9] shows that this explanation is correct. The Armenians were not massacred spontaneously by the local Moslems; the initiative came entirely from the Central Government at Constantinople, which planned the systematic extermination of the Armenian race in the Ottoman Empire, worked out a uniform method of procedure, despatched simultaneous orders to the provincial officials and gendarmerie to carry it into effect, and cashiered the few who declined to obey. The Armenians were rounded up and deported by regular troops and gendarmes; they were massacred on the road by bands of *chettis*, consisting chiefly of criminals released from prison by the Government for this work;

---

8 Which (for obvious reasons) was printed for private circulation only.

9 Miscellaneous No. 31 (1916).

when the Armenians were gone the Turkish populace was encouraged to plunder their goods and houses, and as the convoys of exiles passed through the villages the best-looking women and children were sold cheap or even given away for nothing to the Turkish peasantry. Naturally the Turkish people accepted the good things the Government offered them, and naturally this reconciled them momentarily to the War.

Thus in the Armenian atrocities the Young Turks made Panislamism and Turkish Nationalism work together for their ends, but the development of their policy shows the Islamic element receding and the Nationalist gaining ground.

"After the deposition of Abd-ul-Hamid," writes the German authority quoted above, "the Committee of Union and Progress reverted more and more to the ex-Sultan's policy. To begin with, a rigorous party tyranny was set up. A power behind the Government got the official executive apparatus into its hand, and the elections to Parliament ceased to be free. The appointment of the highest officials in the Empire and of all the most important servants of the administration was settled by decrees of the Committee. All bills had to be debated first by the Committee and to receive its approval before they came before the Chamber. Public policy was determined by two main considerations: (1) The centralistic idea, which claimed for the Turkish race not merely preponderant but exclusive power in the Empire, was to be carried to its logical consequences; (2) The Empire was to be established on a purely Islamic foundation. Turkish Nationalism and the Panislamic Idea precluded *a priori* any equality of treatment for the various races and religions of the Empire, and any movement which looked for the salvation of the Empire in the decentralisation or autonomy of its various parts was branded as high treason. The nationalistic and centralistic tendency was directed not merely against the various non-Mohammedan nationalities —Greeks, Armenians, Syrians, and Jews—but also against the non-Turkish Mohammedan nations—Arabs, Mohammedan Syrians, Kurds, and the Shia element in the population. An idol of 'Pan-Turkism' was erected, and all non-Turkish elements in the population were subjected to the harshest measures. The rigorous action which this policy prescribed against the Albanians, who were mostly Mohammedans and had been thorough loyalists till then, led to the loss of almost the whole of European Turkey. The same policy has provoked insurrections in the Arab half of the Empire, which a series of campaigns has failed to suppress. The conflict with the Arab element continues"—this was written in 1916—"though the 'Holy War' has forced it to a certain extent into the background."

"The conflict with the Arabs"—that has been the worst folly of the Young Turkish politicians, and it will perhaps be the most powerful solvent of the Empire which the Osmanlis have misgoverned so long. It is the inevitable consequence of the camarilla government and the Pan-Turkish chauvinism for which the Committee of Union and Progress has come to stand.

The Committee consists by its statutes of Turks alone, and the election even of one Arab was vetoed.[10] Tekin Alp informs us that

"The portfolio of the Minister of Trade and Agriculture, which has been in the hands of Greeks and Armenians since the time of the Constitution, and was lately given to a Christian Arab, has at last been handed over to the Constantinople deputy Ahmed Nasimi Bey, who

---

10   Memorial of the German authority cited above.

joined with Ziya Goek Alp in laying the foundations of the Turkish Movement immediately after the proclamation of the Constitution. With one exception the members of the Cabinet are all imbued with the same ideas and principles."

The Armenian deportations gave the Committee an opportunity of tightening its hold over the provincial officials as well. Valis who refused to carry out the orders were superseded if they were strong-minded enough to persist; but more often they were browbeaten by the leaders of the local Young Turk organisations, or even by their own subordinates, and let things go their way. Ways and means of packing the administration with their own henchmen had been discussed by the Committee already in their congress of October, 1911, and they had defined their policy then in the following remarkable resolutions:[11]

"The formation of new parties in the Chamber or in the country must be suppressed and the emergence of new 'liberal ideas' prevented. Turkey must become a really Mohammedan country, and Moslem ideas and Moslem influence must be preponderant. Every other religious propaganda must be suppressed. The existence of the Empire depends on the strength of the Young Turkish Party and the suppression of all antagonistic ideas....

"Sooner or later the complete Ottomanisation of all Turkish subjects must be effected; it is clear, however, that this can never be attained by persuasion, but that we must resort to armed force. The character of the Empire must be Mohammedan, and respect must be secured for Mohammedan institutions and traditions. Other nationalities must be denied the right of organisation, for decentralisation and autonomy are trea-

---

11   Quoted by the German authority cited above.

son to the Turkish Empire. *The nationalities are a quantite negligeable. They can keep their religion but not their language. The propagation of the Turkish language is one of the sovereign means of confirming the Mohammedan supremacy and assimilating the other elements."*

The confusion of aims in these two paragraphs reveals the direction in which Young Turkish policy has been travelling. Religion is now secondary to language, and the precedence still given to the Islamic formula is only in apparent contradiction to this, for Mohammedan supremacy is equated with the Turkish National Idea. Such a version of Panislamism leaves no room for an Arab race under Ottoman rule, and the "Panturanian" address given by the Turkish Professor at the Military College in Constantinople had a sequel which showed the Arabs what they, too, had to expect from Turkey's entrance into the War.

There were Arabs among the officers whom the Professor was addressing, and one of them ventured to protest.

"All Ottomans are not Turks," he said, "and if the Empire were to be considered purely Turkish, then all the non-Turkish elements would be foreign to it, instead of being living members of the political body known as the Ottoman Empire, fighting the common fight for it and for Islam."

To this the Professor is reported to have replied:

"Although you are an Arab, yet you and your race are subject to Turkey. Have not the Turks colonised your country, and have they not conquered it by the sword? The Ottoman State, which you plead, is nothing but a social trick, to which you resort in order to attain your ends. As to religion, it has no connexion with politics. We shall soon march forward in the name of Turkey and the Turkish flag, casting aside religion, as it is only a personal and secondary question. You and your nation must realise that you are Turks, and that there is no such thing as Arab nationality and an Arab fatherland."

It is said that the Arab officers present handed in a joint protest to the Minister of War, asking for the Professor's dismissal, and that Enver Bey's answer was to have them all sent to the front-line trenches.

Certainly the Turkish Nationalists have not concealed their attitude towards the Arabs since the War began.

"The Arab lands," writes Djelal Noury Bey in a recently-published work, "and above all Irak[12] and Yemen, must become Turkish colonies in which we shall spread our own language, so that at the right moment we may make it the language of religion. It is a peculiarly imperious necessity of our existence for us to Turkise the Arab lands, for the particularistic idea of nationality is awaking among the younger generation of Arabs, and already threatens us with a great catastrophe. Against this we must be forearmed."

And Ahmed Sherif Bey, again, has written as follows in the *Tanin:*

"The Arabs speak their own language and are as ignorant of Turkish as if their country were not a dependency of Turkey. It is the business of the *Porte* to make them forget their own language and to impose upon them instead that of the nation which rules them. If the Porte loses sight of this duty it will be digging its grave with its own hands, for if the Arabs do not forget their language, their history, and their customs, they

---

12   The Vilayets of Basra and Bagdad.

will seek to restore their ancient empire on the ruins of Ottomanism and of Turkish rule in Asia."

A Turkish pamphleteer wrote that "the Arabs have been a misfortune to Turkey," and that "a Turkish conqueror's war-horse is better than the Prophet of any other nation." This pamphlet was distributed in the Caucasus at the Ottoman Government's expense as Turkish propaganda.

But the best proof of the Young Turks' intentions towards the Arabs is their actual conduct in the Arab provinces of their Empire. In the spring of 1916 an Arab who had escaped from Syria published some facts in the Egyptian Press which the Turkish censorship had previously managed to conceal.[13] Business was ruined, because the Turks had confiscated all gold and forced the people to accept depreciated paper; the population was starving, and the Turks had prohibited the American colony at Beirut from organising relief; the national susceptibilities of the inhabitants were outraged in petty ways—the railway tickets, for instance, were no longer printed in Arabic, but only in Turkish and German; and spies were active in denouncing the least manifestations of disaffection. A Turkish court-martial was sitting in the Lebanon, and at the time our informant left Syria it had 240 persons under arrest, 180 of them on political charges. These prisoners were the leading men of Syria—Christians and Moslems without distinction; for in Syria, as in Armenia, the Turks put the leaders out of the way before they attacked the nation as a whole; most of the Syrian bishops had been deported

---

13 See the journal *Al-Mokattam* of Cairo, 30th March, 31st March, 1st April, 1916 (English translation in the form of a pamphlet: "Syria during March, 1916," printed by Sir Joseph Causton and Sons Ltd., 1916).

or driven into hiding; by the beginning of March, 1916, it was reckoned that 816 Arabs in Syria and 117 in Mesopotamia had already been condemned to death with the confiscation of their property. A Turkish officer, taking our informant for a Turk too, remarked to him: "Those Arabs wish to get rid of us and are secretly in sympathy with our enemies, but we mean to get rid of them ourselves before they have any chance of translating their sympathy into action." This caps what a Turkish gendarme in Armenia said to a Danish sister serving with the German Red Cross: "First we kill the Armenians, then the Greeks, then the Kurds."[14] Every non-Turkish nationality in the Ottoman Empire is threatened with extermination.

But the aims of Turkish Nationalists are not limited by the Ottoman frontiers. If they are resolved to clear their Empire of every non-Turkish element, that is only a step towards extending it over everything Turkish that lies outside. The Turks have not only aliens to get rid of, but an irredenta to win.

"The Ottoman Turks," Tekin Alp reminds his readers, "now only represent a tenth of the whole Turkish nation. There are now sixty to seventy million Turkish subjects of various states in the world, who should succeed in giving the nation an important place among the other Powers. Unfortunately, there is no connexion between the separate groups, which are distributed over great tracts of land. Their aspirations and national institutions still divide them.... Now that the Ottoman Turks have awakened from their sleep of centuries they do not only think of themselves, but hasten to save the other parts of their race who are living in slavery or ignorance....

---

14   Miscellaneous No. 31 (1916), p. 253.

"Turkish irredentism may be directed towards material or moral reforms according to circumstances. If the geographical position favours the venture, the Turks can free their brothers from foreign rule. In the other case, they can carry it on on moral or intellectual lines.

"Irredentism, which other nations may regard as a luxury—though often a very terrible and costly one—is a political and social necessity for the Turks.... If all the Turks in the world were welded into one huge community, a strong nation would be formed, worthy to take an important place among the other nations of the world."[15]

This may be a dream, but the Young Turks have used the political and military resources of the Ottoman Empire to make it a reality. At the congress of 1911 it was resolved that "immigration from the Caucasus and Turkestan must be promoted, land found for the immigrants, and the Christians hindered from acquiring real estate." Turkey was first to be reinforced by the Turks abroad; in the European War she was to strike out as their liberator. The day after their declaration of war the Young Turkish Government issued a proclamation in which the following sentences occur:

"Our participation in the world war represents the vindication of our national ideal. The ideal of our nation and people leads us towards the destruction of our Muscovite enemy, in order to obtain thereby a natural frontier to our empire, which should include and unite all branches of our race."

When war broke out the "Dashnaktzagan"—the Armenian parliamentary party in the Ottoman Empire—were in congress at Erzerum. A deputation of Young

---

15 *Thoughts on the Nature and Plan of a Greater Turkey.*

Turk propagandists[16] presented themselves, and urged the Armenians to join them in raising a general insurrection in Caucasia. They sketched their proposed partition of Russian territory; the Tatars[17] were to have this, the Georgians that, the Armenians this other; autonomy for the new provinces under Ottoman suzerainty was to be the reward for co-operation. The Dasknaktzagan had always worked with the Young Turks in internal politics, but they refused to join them in this aggressive venture. The Ottoman Armenians, they said, would do their duty as Ottoman subjects during the war, but they advised the Government to preserve peace if that were still possible.[18] But the Turks were past reason, and their Army was already on the move. The main body crossed the Russian frontier; a second force invaded Northern Persia, and penetrated as far as Tabriz. Tabriz is the capital of Azerbaijan, a province where the majority of the population is Turkish by language; and beyond, across the River Aras, lies the Russian province of Baku, also containing a large Turkish-speaking population and the vital oilfields. The Turkish plan of campaign was frustrated by the brilliant Russian victory of Sarikamysh. By the end of January, 1915, the Turkish Army was back within its own frontiers, and in this quarter it has not again advanced beyond them. But the Young Turks' irredentist ambitions have remained in being. During their brief occupation of Northern Persia they did their best to wipe out the Syriac element in the population—the Nestorian Christians of Urmia. Their plan was to get rid of all the non-Turkish peoples which separate the Turks of Anatolia from the Turks of Baku and Azerbai-

---

16 Emir Hechmat, their chief, subsequently went to Hamadan in Persia and organised guerilla bands there.

17 *i.e.,* the Turkish-speaking population in the Russian Caucasus.

18 Miscellaneous No. 31 (1916), p. 80.

jan, and this was the second motive of the Armenian deportations, which they put in hand a month or two after their military projects had failed.

The Turkish Irredentists propose, in fact, to gain their ends by bloodshed and terrorism. Tekin Alp (like most Turkish publicists and politicians since 1908) is a Macedonian,[19] and is profoundly impressed by the methods which the other nationalities there employed to the discomfiture of the Turks themselves.

"Observers," he writes, "who, like myself, are Macedonians, and, like myself, had ample opportunity of gaining an intimate knowledge of the irredentist propaganda of the Bulgars, Greeks, Serbs, and Vlachs, are able to judge the significance of this striving after a national ideal, and how sweet and inspiring it is to go through the greatest dangers for such a cause. This is best illustrated by a few living examples" (which he proceeds to give)....

Macedonia is soaked in blood. Atrocities were committed here the mere thought of which makes one's hair stand on end. Nevertheless, the leaders of robber bands and members of the terrible irredentist organisations were not regarded by the public as wild robbers, but as heroes fighting for the unity of the nation.

"Will the Young Turks emulate the self-sacrifice of these men?"

Russia and Persia are the fields marked out for such activity:

"In some places ordinary propaganda is sufficient, but in hotly-contested territory recourse is to be had to the

---

19   And, like other Young Turks, a Jew ("Tekin Alp" being a *nom de plume*).

more violent measures used in Macedonia. The neighbouring land of Persia is without doubt the best of all countries with Turkish population for spreading the new ideas, and it has been found that simple propaganda is amply sufficient to produce a satisfactory effect on this fruitful soil."

In Persia, Tekin Alp reckons, one-third of the population is of Turkish blood. He passes these Turkish elements in review, and concludes that "the spirit of the administration is Turkish, and also the leading spirit of Persian civilisation, even though these be clothed in Persian guise"—for at present the tables are turned. "All those Turkish warriors and heroes, Shahs and Grand Viziers, thinkers and scholars, have lost their Turkish consciousness and have become assimilated to the Persians in writing, speech, and literature." Even the compact two millions and a half of Turkish-speaking Azerbaijanis will write letters only in Persian, and will not read a Turkish newspaper. He omits the most important fact—that these Turks of Persia are Shias like their Persian fellow-countrymen, while the "Mohammedan institutions and traditions" for which the Ottoman Turks are pledged by the Young Turk Party to "secure respect" are those of the Sunni persuasion. But then Turkish Nationalism depends upon ignoring religion. Tekin Alp sets out confidently to give the Turks in Persia "a Turkish soul." His model is the Rumanian propaganda among the Vlachs in Macedonia, and his expectations are great:

"There is no power in Persia to put down such a movement, because it could do no harm to anyone. The nationalisation of the Persian Turks would even be a great and unexpected help to the Persian Government.... Persia would be situated with regard to the Turkish Government as Bavaria towards Prussia."

And this is only a stage towards a higher goal:

"The united Turks should form the centre of gravity of the world of Islam. The Arabs of Egypt, Morocco and Tunisia, the Persians, Afghans, etc., must enjoy complete independence in their own affairs, but outwardly the world of Islam must present a perfectly united front."

The Arabs of North Africa and the Shias of Iran can appraise the "independence" held out to them by the "unity" which Turkish Nationalism has been presenting already to Syria and Irak, the Yemen and the Hedjaz.

But Tekin Alp deals even less tenderly with Russia. In explaining the bond of interest between Turkish Nationalism and Germany he remarks that

"The Pan-Turkish aspirations cannot come to their full development and realisation until the Muscovite monster is crushed, because the very districts which are the object of Turkish Irredentism—Siberia, the Caucasus, the Crimea, Afghanistan, etc.—are still directly or indirectly under Russian rule."

The "et cetera" proves to be nothing less than the province of Kazan:

"The alluvial plains of the Volga and the Kama, in European Russia, are inhabited by four or five million Turks.... The Northern Turks are not indeed superior to the Ottoman Turks, but must not therefore be underrated. Their progressive economic and social organisation is in every way a great help to the national movement.

"If," he concludes, "the Russian despotism is, as we hope, to be destroyed by the brave German, Austrian, and Turkish Armies, thirty to forty million Turks will receive their independence. With the ten million Ottoman Turks this will form a nation of fifty million, advancing towards a great civilisation which may perhaps be compared to that of Germany, in that it will have the strength and energy to rise ever higher. In some ways it will be even superior to the degenerate French and English civilisations."

This Nationalism, which dominates Turkey's present, has also decided the question of her future. If such a movement has taken possession of the Osmanlis, the Osmanlis must lose possession of their Empire. Turkish Nationalism now directs the Ottoman Government, wields its pretensions, is master within its frontiers; and how does it use its mastery? To make a hell of Armenia and Syria, and to plot out new Macedonias in Persia and the heart of Russia. Thus Turkish Nationalism shows where the Turk is intolerable and must go, but it also shows where he has some right to stay.

There are innocent and constructive elements in it, as in all movements of the kind. As in Europe, it has forced open the Dead Hand of the Church. Under its influence the Ministry of *Evkaf,* which holds the enormous religious endowments of Turkey in trust, has turned its funds to the founding of a national bank and library, and the subsidising of a national architecture. It has also started elementary schools, like the voluntary schools supported by the Christian nationalities, in aid of the Ministry of Education; and it has taken up the reform of the Moslem seminaries *(Medresses),* which have been one of the strongholds of Turkish reaction. The welfare of Turkish students is a concern of the Nationalist society called *Turk Ujaghi* (the Turkish Family), founded in 1912, and now possessing sixteen branches in various provincial towns

of Anatolia—only Turks may be members—with af-
filiated societies in the Caucasus and Turkestan. The
Turk Ujaghi organises lantern lectures, lectures on
mediaeval Anatolian art, and even lectures by a Turkish lady on Panturanianism and woman's rights—she
is said to have had Khodjas[20] in her audience, and, if so,
this certainly shows an unheard-of openness to new
ideas on the part of the "Islamji." Another society, the
Turk Gueji (Turkish Strength), encourages physical
culture like the Slavonic *Sokols,* and there are *Izdjis,*
or Turkish Boy-Scouts, under Enver Bey's patronage,
who take "Turanian" scout-names, blazon the White
Wolf of Turkish paganism on their flags, and cheer, it
is said, not for the "Caliph" or the "Padishah," but for
the "Khakan."

This jumble of efforts, half-admirable and half-absurd,
will justify Turkish Nationalism if it brings about the
regeneration of the Anatolian peasantry. The Anato-
lians have suffered as much from the Ottoman dominion as any of the races which have come under its yoke.
They have paid for Ottoman Imperialism with their
blood and physique; their villages have been ravaged
by the syphilis of the garrison towns, and the wider the
frontiers of the Empire the further from their homes
the Anatolian soldiers have died—in the Yemen, in Al-
bania, in Irak, on the snow-covered Armenian plateau.
Two things are necessary for Anatolia's salvation—the
limitation of the Turkish State to the lands inhabited
by its Turkish-speaking population, and the replace-
ment of the mongrel Osmanli bureaucracy by a cleaner
and more democratic political order. If the Allies can
compass this, they may claim without hypocrisy to
have liberated another nationality; for Anatolia will
be reborn on the day of its escape from the Ottoman

---

20 Moslem *religieux.*

chrysalis as truly as were Serbia and Greece and Rumania and Bulgaria.

The beginnings will be difficult, as they have been in the Balkans. Whatever frontiers a Turkish National State may receive, they cannot be drawn without including non-Turkish elements—racial geography is nowhere very simple between Bagdad and Vienna—and in view of what the Turk's racial minorities have suffered during the War and before it, those left to him hereafter must be safeguarded by stringent guarantees—far more stringent than the Capitulations, which, for that matter, protected none but the nationals of foreign Powers. The Capitulations are a problem in themselves. They were repudiated by the Young Turkish Government at the beginning of the War, as well as the conventions regulating the customs tariff. It is difficult to see how the Peace Conference can pass over flagrant violations of international treaties, and the Nationalists' contention that Turkish justice has been brought up to a European standard will not bear examination; on the contrary, the Young Turkish congress of 1911 passed a resolution that "the reorganisation of the administration of justice was less important than the abolition of the Capitulations." These difficulties, however, might be settled with a new and better Anatolian government; and as for the racial question, with time and guaranteed tolerance for religion it might solve itself, for there is a rude vitality in the Turkish language, and the Greek and Armenian minorities in Central Anatolia have been gradually adopting it in place of their native speech, though this tendency is now being counteracted by the spread of national schools among the scattered outposts of the two nationalities in the interior.

III

THE FUTURE

With these suggestions, Anatolia and Turkish Nationalism may be dismissed from our survey. Shorn of their pretensions in Armenia and the countries south of Taurus, the Turks may experiment in the art of government without the tragedies which their present domination has brought upon mankind. The other lands and peoples of Western Asia, when they have ceased to be "Turkey," will be restored once more to the civilised world. What forces will shape their growth? Not, even indirectly, the discrowned Turk, for if he were not banned by his crimes he would still be doomed by his incapacity.

The relative qualities of the different Near Eastern races are not in doubt. A German teacher in the German Technical School at Aleppo, who resigned his appointment as a protest against the Armenian atrocities in 1915, thus records his personal judgment in an open letter to the *Reichstag*:[21]

---

21   Ein Wort an die Berufenen Vertreter des Deutschen Volkes: Eindrucke eines deutschen Oberlehrers aus der Tuerkei, von

"The Young Turk is afraid of the Christian nationalities—Armenians, Syrians and Greeks—on account of their cultural and economic superiority, and he sees in their religion a hindrance to Turkifying them by peaceful means. They must therefore be exterminated or converted to Islam by force. The Turks do not suspect that in so doing they are sawing off the branch on which they are sitting themselves. Yet who is to help Turkey forward if not the Greeks, Armenians, and Syrians, who constitute more than a quarter of the population of the Empire? The Turks, *the least gifted of the races living in Turkey,* are themselves only a minority of the population, and are still far behind the Arabs in culture. Where is there any Turkish trade, Turkish handicraft, Turkish industry, Turkish art, Turkish science? They have even borrowed their law and religion from the conquered Arabs, and their language, so far as it has been given literary form.

"We teachers, who have been teaching Greeks, Armenians, Arabs, Turks, and Jews in German schools in Turkey for years, can only pass judgment that of all our pupils the pure Turks are the most unwilling and the least talented. When for once in a way a Turk does achieve something, one can be sure in nine cases out of ten that one is dealing with a Circassian, an Albanian, or a Turk with Bulgarian blood in his veins. From my personal experience I can only prophesy that the Turks proper will never achieve anything in trade, industry, or science.

"We are told now in the German Press about the Turks' hunger for education, and of how they are thronging

---

Dr. Martin Niepage, Oberlehrer an der deutschen Realschule zu Aleppo, z.Zt. Wernigerode. (Printed in the second pamphlet issued by the Swiss Committee for Armenian Relief at Basel; English translation, "The Horrors of Aleppo." London, 1917: Hodder and Stoughton.)

eagerly to learn German. There is even a report of language courses for adults which have been started in Turkey. They have certainly been started, but with what result? One reads of the language course at a technical school which began with twelve Turkish teachers as pupils. Our informant forgets to add, however, that after four lessons only six pupils presented themselves; after five, five; after six, four; and after seven only three, so that after eight lessons the course broke down, through the indolence of the pupils, before it had properly commenced. If the pupils had been Armenians they would have persevered till the end of the school year, learnt industriously, and finished with a respectable mastery of the German language."

From a German teacher who has worked in Turkey for three years this verdict is crushing, and Tekin Alp himself virtually admits the charge. "It is true," he writes, "that the Turkish character is usually lacking in the qualities most essential to trade or economic undertakings, but these may be acquired by a reasonable and methodical training and organisation." The only "organisation" that seems to occur to him is the Boycott, which has been popular with the Turks since the Revolution of 1908.

"The unaccommodating attitude of the Greek Government was sufficient excuse," he remarks, in reference to the Boycott of 1912. "The real motive, however, was the longing of the Turkish nation for independence in their own country. The Boycott, which was at first directed solely against the Greeks, was then extended to the Armenians and other non-Mohammedan circles, and was carried out with undiminished energy. This movement, which lasted in all its rigour for several months, caused the ruin of hundreds of small Greek and Armenian tradesmen.... The systematic and rigorous Boycott is now at an end, but the spirit it created in the people still persists.... It can now be asserted that the movement for restoring the economic life of Turkey is on the right road."

The real effects of the Boycott of 1912 are described by the German authority whose memorial has several times been cited in this article. He tells us how, under the patronage of the Young Turkish Government, associations were formed which intimidated the Moslem peasants into buying from them, when they came to market, instead of from the Christians with whom they had formerly dealt.

"The peasants came to their old dealers," the memorial continues, "lamented their fate, and asked their advice as to how they could save themselves from the hands of their fellow-countrymen. They were delighted when at last the Boycott came to an end and they could once more buy from Greeks and Armenians, where they were well served and got good value for their money."

If the Turkish Nationalists had confined themselves to economic weapons, the Turks' economic ineptitude would have prevented them from doing serious harm; but by abusing the political and military powers of the Ottoman State to perpetrate the recent atrocities they have struck a mortal blow at the prosperity of Western Asia.

"In the whole of Asia Minor, with perhaps one or two exceptions," the same German authority states, "there is not a single pure Turkish firm engaged in foreign trade.... The extermination of the Armenian population means not only the loss of from 10 to 25 per cent. of the total population of Anatolia,[22] but, what is most

---

22   The writer includes Armenia under this term.

serious, the elimination of those elements in the population which are the most highly developed economically and have the greatest capacity for civilisation...."

And this is the universal judgment of those in a position to know.

"The result of the deportations," the American Consul at Aleppo declares in an official report,[23] "is that, as 90 per cent. of the commerce of the interior is in the hands of the Armenians, the country is facing ruin. The great bulk of business being done on credit, hundreds of prominent business men other than Armenians are facing bankruptcy. There will not be left in the places evacuated a single tanner, moulder, blacksmith, tailor, carpenter, clay-worker, weaver, shoemaker, jeweller, pharmacist, doctor, lawyer, or any of the professional people or tradesmen, with very few exceptions, and the country will be left in a practically helpless state."

The German memorialist presses the indictment:

"You cannot become a merchant by murdering one. You cannot master a handicraft if you smash its tools. A sparsely-populated country does not become more productive if it destroys its most industrious population. You do not advance the progress of civilisation if you drive into the desert, as the scapegoat for decades and centuries of wasted opportunities, the element in your population which shows the greatest economic ability, the greatest progressiveness in education, and the greatest energy in every respect, and which was fitted by nature to build the bridge between East and West. You only corrupt your own sense of right if you tread the rights of others under foot. The popularity of an unpopular war may temporarily be promoted

---

23   Dated 3rd Aug., 1915: See Miscellaneous No. 31 (1916), p. 548.

among the Turkish masses by the destruction and spo-
liation of the non-Mohammedan elements—the Armenians most of all, but also, in part, the Syrians, Greeks,
Maronites, and Jews—but thoughtful Mohammedans,
when they realise the whole damage which the Empire
has sustained, will lament the economic ruin of Turkey most bitterly, and will come to the conclusion that
the Turkish Government has lost infinitely more than
it can ever win"—it is a German writing—"by victories
at the front."

"We may call it political necessity or what not," declared
an American travelling in Anatolia during the deportations of 1915, "but in essence it is a nominally ruling class,
jealous of a more progressive race, striving by methods
of primitive savagery to maintain the leading place." [24]

What forces will be released in Western Asia when
the Turk has met his fate? Who will repair the ruin he
leaves behind?

The Germans? They have been penetrating Turkey economically for the last thirty years. They have organised regular steamship services between German and
Turkish ports, multiplied the volume of Turco-German
trade, and extended their capital investments, particularly in the Ottoman Debt and the construction of railways. In 1881, when the Debt was first placed under
international administration, Germany held only 4.7
per cent., of it, and was the sixth in importance of Turkey's creditors; by 1912 she held 20 per cent., and was
second only to France. [25] Her railway enterprises, more
ambitious than those of any other foreign Power, have

---

24 Miscellaneous No. 31 (1916), p. 413.
25 "Die deutsch-tuerkeschen Wirtschaftsbeziehungen," by Dr.
Kurt Wiedenfeld, Professor of the Political Sciences at the
University of Halle. (Duncker and Humblot, 1915).

brought valuable concessions in their train—harbour works at Haidar Pasha and Alexandretta, irrigation works in the Konia oasis and the Adana plain, and the prospect, when the Bagdad Railway reaches the Tigris, of tapping the naphtha deposits of Kerkuk.[26] Dr. Rohrbach, the German specialist on the Near East, forecasts the profits of the Bagdad Railway from the results of Russian railway-building in Central Asia. He prophesies the cultivation of cotton, in the regions opened up by the line, on a scale which will cover an appreciable part of the demands of German industry, and will open a corresponding market for German wares among the new cotton-growing population.[27] "Yet the decisive factor in the Bagdad Railway," he counsels his German readers, "is not to be found in these economic considerations but in another sphere."

Dr. Wiedenfeld drives this home.

"Germany's relation to Turkey," his monograph begins, "belies the doctrine that all modern understandings and differences between nations have an economic origin. We are certainly interested in the economic advancement of Turkey ... but in setting ourselves to make Turkey strong we have been influenced far more by our political interests as a State among States *(das politische, das staatlich-machtliche Interesse)*. Even our economic activity has primarily served this aim, and has in fact originated to a large extent in the purely politico-military problems *(aus den unmittelbaren Machtaufgaben)* which confronted the Turkish Government. Exclusively economic considerations play a very subordinate part in Turco-German relations.... Our common political aims, and Germany's interest in

---

26 "Die Bagdadbahn," by Dr. Paul Rohrbach (Berlin, 1911), pp. 43, 44.

27 "Die Bagdadbahn," pp. 49, 50.

keeping open the land-route to the Indian Ocean, will make it more than ever imperative for us to strengthen Turkey economically with all our might, and to put her in a position to build up, on independent economic foundations, a body politic strong enough to withstand all external assaults. The means will still be economic; the goal will be of a political order."[28]

And Dr. Rohrbach formulates the political goal with startling precision. After twelve pages of disquisition on recent international diplomacy he brings his thesis to this point: the Bagdad Railway links up with the railways of Syria, and

"The importance of the Syrian railway system lies in this, that, if the need arose, it would be the direct instrument for the exercise of pressure upon England ... supposing that German-Austro-Turkish co-operation became necessary in the direction of Egypt."

Written as it was in 1911, this is a remarkable anticipation of Turkish strategic railway-building since the outbreak of war; but it is infinitely remote in purpose from the economic regeneration of Western Asia, and even when the German publicists reckon in economic values they generally betray their political design.

"The special point for Germany," Dr. Wiedenfeld lays down, in discussing the agricultural possibilities of the Ottoman territories, "is that to a large extent crops can be grown here which supplement our own economic resources in important respects.... In peace time, of course, no one would think of transporting goods of such bulk as agricultural products any way but by sea;

---

28 The author rubs in his point in his concluding section: "All economic measures we may take in Turkey are only a means to an end, not an end in themselves" (p. 77).

but the War has impressed on us with brutal clearness the value for us of being able on occasions of extreme necessity to import cotton from Turkey by land."

Thus Germany's economic activity in Turkey has been not for prosperity but for power, not for peace but for war. In developing Turkey, Germany is simply developing the "Central Europe" scheme of a military combine self-contained economically and challenging the world in arms.[29] Germany is concerned with Turkey, not for her splendid past and future, but for her miserable present; for Turkey—as she is, and only as she is—is a vital chequer on the chess-board where Germany has been playing her game of world power, or "des staatlich-machtlichen Interessens," as Dr. Wiedenfeld would say. Therefore Germany does not eye the lands and peoples under Ottoman dominion with a view to their common advantage and her own. She selects a "piece" among them which she can keep under her thumb and so control the square. Abd-ul-Hamid was her first pawn, and when the Young Turk Party swept him off the board she adopted them and their colour;[30] for by hook or by crook, through this agency or that, Turkey had to be commanded or Germany's play was spoilt.

Germany's control over Turkey depends upon the maintenance of a corrupt minority in power—too weak and corrupt to remain in it without Germany's guarantee, and corrupt enough, when secured in it, to put it at Germany's disposal. A free hand at home in return

---

29 Wiedenfeld's monograph is a *sonderabdruck* from the two volumes of studies on the "Wirtschaftliche Annaherung zwischen dem deutschen Reich u. seinen Verbundeten," edited by Heinrich Herkner and published by the *Verein fur Sozialpolitik,* which preaches Naumann's creed.

30 Just as, by a more gradual process, the Magyar Oligarchy, rather than the Hapsburg Dynasty, has become the instrument of German control over Austria-Hungary.

for servitude in diplomacy and war—the deal is called "Hegemony," and is as old as Ancient Greece. By her hegemony over the Ottoman Government Germany threatens the British and Russian Empires from all the Ottoman frontiers; and with the free hand that is their price the Young Turks inflict on all lands and peoples within those frontiers whatever evils conduce to the maintenance of their pretensions.

As Rohrbach and Wiedenfeld point out, this political understanding underlies all Germany's economic efforts in Western Asia, and we can see how it has warped them from their proper ends. The track of the Bagdad Railway, for example, has not been selected in the economic interests of the lands and peoples which it ostensibly serves. Dr. Rohrbach himself admits that

"The Anatolian section of the Bagdad Railway cannot be described as properly paying its way. It is otherwise with the" (French) "line from Smyrna to Afiun Kara Hissar, which links the Anatolian Railway with the older railway system in the West.... The parts of Asia Minor which were thickly populated and prosperous in antiquity lie mostly westward of this first section of the Bagdad Railway, round the river-valleys and" (French and English) "railways leading down to the Aegean."

"There are other once-flourishing parts of the peninsula," he continues, "which the Bagdad Railway does not touch at all"—the Vilayet of Sivas and the other Armenian provinces. The original German plan was to carry the Railway through Armenia from Angora to Kharput, but Russia not unnaturally vetoed the construction, so near her Caucasian frontiers, of a line which, by the nature of the Turco-German understanding, must primarily serve strategic ends,[31] and the track was there-

---

31   "Die Bagdadbahn," pp. 29, 33.

fore deflected to the south-east. This took it through the most barren parts of Central Anatolia, and in the next section involved the slow and costly work of tunnelling the Taurus and Amanus mountains.

"If merely economic and not political advantages were taken into account," Dr. Rohrbach concedes, "the question might perhaps be raised whether it would not be better to leave the Anatolian section alone altogether and begin the Bagdad Railway from Seleucia" (on the Syrian coast). "The future export trade in grain, wool, and cotton will in any case do all it can to lengthen the cheap sea-passage and shorten correspondingly the section on which it must pay railway freights. The fact that the route connecting Bagdad with the Mediterranean coast in the neighbourhood of Antioch is the oldest, greatest, and still most promising trade-route of Western Asia is independent of all railway projects."

It is worth remembering that a railway, following this route from the Syrian coast to the Persian Gulf, has more than once been projected by the British Government. As early as the thirties of last century Colonel Chesney was sent out to examine the ground, and in 1867 the proposal was considered by a Committee of the House of Commons. For the economic development of Western Asia it is clearly a better plan, but then Dr. Rohrbach bases the "necessity for the East Anatolian section of the Bagdad Railway" on wholly different grounds.

"The necessity," he declares, "consists in Turkey's military interests, which obviously would be very poorly served" (by German railway enterprise) "if troops could not be transported by train without a break from Bagdad and Mosul to the extremity of Anatolia, and *vice versa*."

The Bagdad Railway is thus acknowledged to be an instrument of strategy for the Germans and for the Turks of domination—for *"vice versa"* means that Turkish troops can be transported at a moment's notice through the tunnels from Anatolia to enforce the Ottoman pretension over the Arab lands. Militarily, these tunnels are the most valuable section of the line; economically, they are the most costly and unremunerative. And the second (and longer) tunnel could still have been dispensed with, if, south of Taurus, the track had been led along the Syrian coast. "Economic interests and considerations of expense," Wiedenfeld concedes,[32] "argued strongly for the latter course, but—fortunately, as we must admit today—the military point of view prevailed." Thus the Turco-German understanding prevented the Bagdad Railway first from beginning at a port on the Mediterranean coast, and then from touching the coast at all.[33] "The spine of Turkey," as German writers are fond of calling it, distorts the natural articulation of Western Asia.

Nemesis has overtaken the Germans in the Armenian deportations—a "political end" of Turkish Nationalism which swept away the "economic means" towards Germany's subtler policy. A month or two before the outbreak of war Dr. Rohrbach stated, in a public lecture, that

"Germany has an important interest in effecting and maintaining contact with the Armenian nation. We have set before ourselves the necessary and legitimate aim of spreading and enrooting German influence in

---

32 Page 23.

33 Except by a branch line from Adana to Alexandretta, Rohrbach (pp. 27, 36, 37) laments the economic drawbacks of this strategic necessity.

Turkey, not only by military missions and the construction of railways, but also by the establishment of intellectual relations, by the work of German *Kultur*—in a word, by moral conquests; and we are determined, by pacific means, to reach an amicable understanding with the Turks and the other nations in the Turkish Empire. Our ulterior object in this is to strengthen the Turkish Empire internally with the aid of German science, education, and training, and for this work the Armenians are indispensable."

A few months later Germany, as part price of Turkey's intervention in the War, had to leave the Young Turks a "free hand" to exterminate the nation which was the indispensable instrument of her Turkish policy. On the 9th August, 1915, the German Ambassador at Constantinople handed in a formal protest against the deportations, in which his Government "declined all responsibility for the consequences which might result." On the 11th January, 1916, in the German Reichstag, the Chief of the Political Department of the Foreign Office replied to a question from Dr. Liebknecht that "an exchange of views about the reaction of these measures upon the population was taking place," and that "further information could not be given." And while Germany was maintaining this "correct attitude" before the world, she was assisting in Turkey at the destruction of her own work.

Even the atrocities of 1909 had damaged the economic prospects of the Adapa district from which Dr. Rohrbach[34] hoped so much, for

"The first thing the Turkish peasants did was to destroy all the steam-ploughs and nearly all the threshing machines (there were over a hundred of them) which the

---

34 "Bagdadbahn," p.60.

Armenian villagers had imported for the cultivation of the Civilian plain." [35]

By the atrocities of 1915 the economic life of Western Asia was completely ruined, and the fruits of German enterprise were swept away in the flood.

"I have before me," writes our German memorialised, "a list of the customers of a single Constantinople firm of importers which places its orders principally in Germany and Austria. The accounts which this firm has outstanding amount to date to L13,922 (Turkish), owing from 378 customers in 42 towns of the interior. In consequence of the Armenian deportations these debts are no longer recoverable. The 378 customers, with all their employees, goods, and assets, have vanished from the face of the earth. Any of the owners that are still alive are now beggars on the borders of the Arabian desert."

At Urfa, after the atrocities of 1896, philanthropists of all nations had founded orphanages and started native industries. Attached to the German orphanage there was a carpet factory, with dyeing vats and a spinnery, which Dr. Rohrbach, [36] after personal investigation, describes as "an institution to be welcomed as unreservedly from the national as from the humanitarian point of view."

"The factory," he remarks, "not only provides work and bread for 400 persons, but has transplanted one of the most profitable and promising industries of the East into the sphere traversed by the German Railway, where German interests are predominant."

He prophesies that the whole carpet industry of Western Asia, "from which English and other foreign firms

---

35   The German memorialised.
36   "Bagdadbahn," pp. 39, 40.

in Smyrna now draw such enormous profits," will soon be concentrated round Urfa in German hands. From Armenia's evil, apparently, springs Germany's good—but in 1911 Dr. Rohrbach did not foresee the catastrophe of 1915.

"For the rise of the carpet industry," our German memorialised writes, "Turkey has to thank capitalists and exporters who are almost all Armenians, Greeks, Jews, or Europeans. Like the cotton cultivation introduced by Germany into Cilicia, this carpet industry, in the eastern provinces, has been deprived of the hands essential to it by the Armenian deportations."

Eye-witnesses at Urfa describe how the Armenian community there was massacred in 1915—the third time in twenty years, and this time to extinction—and it points the irony of the situation that the Turkish guns were served by German artillerymen.[37]

"I have nothing to say," writes Dr. Niepage, the German teacher from Aleppo, "about the opinion of the German officers in Turkey. I often noticed among them an ominous silence or a convulsive effort to change the subject, when any German of warm feelings and independent judgment talked in their presence of the fearful sufferings of the Armenians."

This moral bankruptcy is more fatal to the future of Germany in Western Asia than all the material havoc which the Armenian deportations have caused. For Dr. Niepage is convinced that the blood of the Armenians will be on Germany's head:

---

37 Miscellaneous No. 31 (1916), p. 530. Major Count Wolf von Wolfskahl, who served as adjutant to Fakhri Pasha in the Turkish "punitive expedition" against Urfa, is mentioned as particularly guilty by a trustworthy neutral resident in Syria.

"'The teaching of the Germans,' is the simple Turk's explanation, ... and more sensitive Mohammedans, Turks and Arabs alike, cannot believe that their own Government has ordered these horrors. They lay all excesses at the Germans' door, for the Germans, during the War, are regarded as Turkey's schoolmasters in everything. The mollahs declare in the mosques that the German officers, and not the Sublime Porte, have ordered the maltreatment and extermination of the Armenians.... Others say: 'Perhaps the German Government has its hands tied by certain agreements defining its powers, or perhaps it is not an opportune moment for intervention.'

"Our presence had no ameliorating effect, and what we could do ourselves was negligible.... The abusive epithet 'Giaur' is heard once more by German ears....

"We think it our duty to draw attention to the fact that our educational work in Turkey forfeits its moral basis and the natives' esteem, if the German Government is not in a position to prevent the brutalities inflicted here upon the wives and children of murdered Armenians.

"The writer considers it out of the question that the German Government, if it seriously desired to stem the tide of destruction in this eleventh hour, would find it impossible to bring the Turkish Government to reason....

"If we persist in treating the massacres of Christians as an internal affair of Turkey, which is only important to us because it ensures us the Turks' friendship, then we must change the orientation of our German *Kulturpolitik*. We must stop sending German teachers to Turkey, and we teachers must give up telling our pupils in Turkey about German poets and philosophers,

German culture and German ideals, to say nothing of German Christianity.

"Three years ago I was sent by the Foreign Office as higher-grade teacher to the German Technical School at Aleppo. The Prussian Provincial School Board at Magdeburg specially enjoined upon me, when I went out, to show myself worthy of the confidence reposed in me in the grant of furlough to take up this post. I should not be fulfilling my duty as a German official and an accredited representative of German culture, if I consented to keep silence in face of the atrocities of which I was a witness, or to look on passively while the pupils entrusted to my charge were driven out into the desert to die of starvation.

"The things of which everybody here has been a witness for months past remain as a stain on Germany's shield in the minds of Oriental nations."

What will be left to Germany in Western Asia after the war? She may keep her trade, though Wiedenfeld confesses that "the exchange of commodities between Germany and Turkey has never attained any really considerable dimensions," and that "the German export trade commands no really staple article whatever of the kind exported by England, Austria, and Russia"—unless we count as such munitions and other materials of war.[38] Except for the last item, this German trade will probably remain and grow; but the German hegemony, based on railway enterprise and reinsured by "moral conquests," will scarcely survive the Ottoman dominion.

Happily there are other representatives of culture, other indigenous nationalities, other possibilities of

---

38 On which Wiedenfeld lays stress, pp. 19, 22.

economic development, which will remain in Western Asia when the Turk and German have gone, and which may be equal to repairing the ruin they will leave behind.

For nearly a century now the American Evangelical Missions have been doing work there which is the greatest conceivable contrast to the German *Kulturpolitik* of the last thirty years. A missionary, sent out to relieve the first pioneers, was given the following instructions by the American Board:

"The object of our missions to the Oriental Churches is, first, to revive the knowledge and spirit of the Gospel among them, and, secondly, by this means to operate upon the Mohammedans.

"The Oriental Churches need assistance from their brethren abroad. Our object is not to subvert them: you are not sent among those Churches to proselytise. Let the Armenian remain an Armenian if he will, the Greek a Greek, the Nestorian a Nestorian, the Oriental an Oriental.

"Your great business is with the fundamental doctrines and duties of the Gospel."[39]

In this spirit the American missionaries have worked. They have had no warships behind them, no diplomatic support, no political ambitions, no economic concessions. As Evangelicals their first step was to translate the Bible into all the living languages and current scripts of the Nearer East. For the Bulgars and Armenians this was the beginning of their modern literature, but the jealousy of the Orthodox and Gregorian clergy was naturally aroused. Native

---

39   "Leavening the Levant," by Rev. J. Greene, D.D. (Beston, 1916: The Pilgrim Press), p. 99.

Protestant Churches formed themselves—not by the missionaries' initiative but on their own. They were trained by the missionaries to self-government, and as they spread from centre to centre they grouped themselves in unions, with annual meetings to settle their common affairs. The missionaries also encouraged them to be self-supporting, and in 1908 the contributions of the Native Churches to the general expenses of the missions were twice as large as those of the American Board.[40] The Ottoman Government recognised its Protestant subjects as a religious corporation *(Millet)* in 1853, and in spite of this the jealousy of the national Churches was overcome. For the work of the Americans was not confined to the new Protestant community. The translation of the Bible led them also into educational work; they laid the foundations of secondary education in Western Asia, and their schools and colleges—still the only institutions of their kind—are attended by Gregorians as well as Protestants, Moslems as well as Christians, Moslem girls as well as boys. As they opened up remoter districts they added medicine to their activities, and their hospitals, like their schools, have been the first in the field. And all this has been built up so unassumingly that its magnitude is hardly realised by the Americans themselves. In the three Turkey Missions, which cover Anatolia and Armenia—the whole of Turkey except the Arab lands—there were, on the eve of the War, 209 American missionaries with 1,299 native helpers, 163 Protestant churches with 15,348 members, 450 schools with 25,922 pupils; Constantinople College and 6 other colleges or high schools for girls; Robert College on the Bosphorus and 9 other colleges for men or boys; and 11 hospitals.

---

40 Excluding, of course, the hospital and educational endowments, and the salaries of the missionaries themselves.

The War, when it came, seemed to sweep away everything. The Protestant Armenians, in spite of a nominal exemption, were deported and massacred like their Gregorian fellow-countrymen; the boys and girls were carried away from the American colleges, the nurses and patients from the hospitals; the empty buildings were "requisitioned" by the Ottoman authorities; the missionaries themselves, in their devoted efforts to save a remnant from destruction, suffered as many casualties from typhus and physical exhaustion as any proportionate body of workers on the European battlefields. The Turkish Nationalists congratulated themselves that the American work in Western Asia was destroyed. In praising a lecture by a member of the German *Reichstag,* who had declared himself "opposed to all missionary activities in the Turkish Empire," a Constantinople newspaper[41] wrote:

"The suppression of the schools founded and directed by ecclesiastical missions or by individuals belonging to enemy nations is as important a measure as the abolition of the Capitulations. Thanks to their schools, foreigners were able to exercise great moral influence over the young men of the country, and they were virtually in charge of its spiritual and intellectual guidance. By closing them the Government has put an end to a situation as humiliating as it was dangerous."

But the missionaries' spirit was something they could not destroy.

"When they deported the Armenians," wrote a missionary, "and left us without work and without friends,

---

41   *Hilal,* 4th April, 1916, quoted in Miscellaneous No. 31 (1916), pp. 654-6.

we decided to come home and get our vacation and be ready to go wherever we could after the War."[42]

After the War the Turks in Anatolia may still be infatuated enough to banish their best friends, but in Armenia, when the Turk has gone, the Americans will find more than their former field; for, in one form or another, Armenia is certain to rise again. The Turks have not succeeded in exterminating the Armenian nation. Half of it lives in Russia, and its colonies are scattered over the world from California to Singapore. Even within the Ottoman frontiers the extermination is not complete, and the Arabian deserts will yield up their living as well as the memory of their dead. The relations of Armenia with the Russian democracy should not be more difficult to settle than those of Finland and Poland; her frontiers cannot be forecast, but they must include the Six Vilayets—so often promised reforms by the Concert of Europe and so often abandoned to the revenges of the Ottoman Government—as well as the Civilian highlands and some outlet to the sea. One thing is certain, that, whatever land is restored to them, the Armenians will turn its resources to good account, for, while their town-dwellers are the merchants and artisans of Western Asia, 80 per cent., of them are tillers of the soil.

What the Americans have done for Armenia has been done for Syria by the French.[43] There are half a million Maronite Catholics in Syria, and since the seventeenth century France has been the protectress of Catholicism in the Near East. In 1864, when there was trouble in Syria and the Maronites were being molested by the Ottoman Government, France landed an army corps

---

42 Miscellaneous No. 31 (1916), p. 309.
43 Though the work of the American Presbyterian Mission at
     Beirut must not be forgotten.

and secured autonomy for the Lebanon under a Christian governor. But French influence is not limited to the Lebanon province. All over Syria there are French clerical, secular, and Judaic schools. Beirut and Damascus, Christian and Moslem—for there is more religious tolerance in Syria than in most Near Eastern countries—are equally under the spell of French civilisation; and France is the chief economic power in the land, for French enterprise has built the Syrian railways. The sufferings of Syria during the War have been described; the Young Turks have confiscated the railways and deprived the Lebanon of its autonomy; even Rohrbach deprecates the fact that "only a few of the higher officials in Syria are chosen from among the natives of the country, while almost all, from the Kaimakam upwards, are sent out from Constantinople," and he attributes to this policy "the feeling against the Turks, which is most acute in Damascus." This is Rohrbach's periphrasis for Arab Nationalism, which will be master in its own house when the Turk has been removed. The future status and boundaries of Syria can no more be forecast than those of Armenia at the present stage of the War; yet here, too, certain tendencies are clear. In some form or other Arab Syria will retain her connection with France, and her growing population will no longer be driven by misgovernment to emigration.

Syrians and Armenians have been emigrating for the last quarter of a century, and during the same period the Jews, whose birthright in Western Asia is as ancient as theirs, have been returning to their native land—not because Ottoman dominion bore less hardly upon them than upon other gifted races, but because nothing could well be worse than the conditions they left behind. For these Jewish immigrants came almost entirely from the Russian Pale, the hearth and hell of modern Jewry. The movement really began after the assassination of Alexander II. in 1881, which threw back reform in Russia for thirty-six years. The Jews were the scapegoats of the reaction. New laws deprived them of their last civil rights, *pogroms* of life itself; they came to Palestine as refugees, and between 1881 and 1914 their numbers there increased from 25,000 to 120,000 souls.

The most remarkable result of this movement has been the foundation of flourishing agricultural colonies. Their struggle for existence has been hard; the pioneers were students or trades-folk of the Ghetto, unused to outdoor life and ignorant of Near Eastern conditions; Baron Edmund de Rothschild financed them from 1884 to 1899 at a loss; then they were taken over by the "Palestine Colonisation Association," which discovered the secrets of success in self-government and scientific methods.

Each colony is now governed by an elective council of inhabitants, with committees for education, police, and the arbitration of disputes, and they have organised co-operative unions which make them independent of middlemen in the disposal of their produce. Their production has rapidly risen in quantity and value, through the industry and intelligence of the average Jewish settler, assisted latterly by an Agricultural Experiment Station at Atlit, near Haifa, which improves the varieties of indigenous crops and acclimatises others.[44] There is a "Palestine Land Development Company" which buys land in big estates and resells it in small lots to individual settlers, and an "Anglo-Palestine Bank" which makes advances to the new settlers when

---

44 See "Zionism and the Jewish Future" (London, 1916: John Murray), pp. 138-170; for the agricultural machinery on the Jewish National Fund's Model Farm at Ben-Shamen, see the Report of the German Vice-Consul at Jaffa for the year 1912.

they take up their holdings. As a result of this enlight-
ened policy the number of colonies has risen to about
forty, with 15,000 inhabitants in all and 110,000 acres
of land, and these figures do not do full justice to the
importance of the colonising movement. The 15,000
Jewish agriculturists are only 12-1/2 per cent. of the
Jewish population in Palestine, and 2 per cent., of the
total population of the country; but they are the most
active, intelligent element, and the only element which
is rapidly increasing. Again, the land they own is only 2
per cent. of the total area of Palestine; but it is between
8 and 14 per cent. of the area under cultivation, and
there are vast uncultivated tracts which the Jews can
and will reclaim, as their numbers grow—both by further colonisation and by natural increase, for the first
generation of colonists have already proved their ability to multiply in the Promised Land. Under this new
Jewish husbandry Palestine has begun to recover its
ancient prosperity. The Jews have sunk artesian wells,
built dams for water storage, fought down malaria by
drainage and eucalyptus planting, and laid out many
miles of roads. In 1890 an acre of irrigable land at
Petach-Tikweh, the earliest colony, was worth L3 12s.,
in 1914, L36, and the annual trade of Jaffa rose from
L760,000 to L2,080,000 between 1904 and 1912. "The
impetus to agriculture is benefiting the whole economic life of the country," wrote the German Vice-Coun-
sul at Jaffa in his report for 1912, and there is no fear
that, as immigration increases, the Arab element will
be crowded to the wall. There are still only two Jewish
colonies beyond Jordan, where the Hauran—under the
Roman Empire a corn-land with a dozen cities—has
been opened up by the railway and is waiting again for
the plough.

But will immigration continue now that the Jew of the
Pale has been turned at a stroke into the free citizen

of a democratic country? Probably it will actually increase, for the Pale has been ravaged as well as liberated during the war, and the Jews of Germany have based an ingenious policy on this prospect, which is expounded thus by Dr. Davis-Trietsch of Berlin:[45]

"According to the most recent statistics about 12,900,000 out of the 14,300,000 Jews in the world speak German or Yiddish *(juedisch-deutsch)* as their mother-tongue.... But its language, cultural orientation, and business relations the Jewish element from Eastern Europe" (the Pale) "is an asset to German influence.... In a certain sense the Jews are a Near Eastern element in Germany and a German element in Turkey."

Germany may not relish her kinship with these lost Teutonic tribes, but Dr. Davis-Trietsch makes a satirical exposure of such scruples:

"It used to be a stock argument against the Jews that 'all nations' regarded them with equal hostility, but the War has brought upon the Germans such a superabundance of almost universal execration that the question which is the most despised of all nations—if one goes, not by justice and equity, but by the violence and extensiveness of the prejudice—might well now be altered to the Germans' disadvantage.

"In this unenviable competition for the prize of hate, Turkey, too, has a word to say, for the unspeakable Turk' is a rhetorical commonplace of English politics."

Having thus isolated the Jews from humanity and pilloried them with the German and the Turk, the writer expounds their function in the Turco-German system:

---

45 "Die Jueden der Tuerkei" (Leipzig, 1915: Veit u. Comp.). Pamphlet No. 8 of the *Deutsches Vorderasienscomitee's* series: "Laender u. Voelker der Tuerkei."

"Hitherto Germany has bothered herself very little about the Jewish emigration from Eastern Europe. People in Germany hardly realised that, through the annual exodus of about 100,000 German-speaking Jews to the United States and England, the empire of the English language and the economic system that goes with it is being enlarged, while a German asset is being proportionately depreciated....

"The War found the Jewry of Eastern Europe in process of being uprooted, and has enormously accelerated the catastrophe. Galicia and the western provinces of Russia, which between them contain many more than half the Jews in the world, have suffered more from the War than any other region. Jewish homes have been broken up by hundreds of thousands, and there is no doubt whatever that, as a result of the War, there will be an emigration of East European Jews on an unprecedented scale....

"The disposal of the East European Jews will be a problem for Germany.... It will no longer do simply to close the German frontiers to them, and in view of the difficulties which would result from a wholesale migration of Eastern Jews into Germany itself, Germans will only be too glad to find a way out in the emigration of these Jews to Turkey—a solution extraordinarily favourable to the interests of all three parties concerned...."

And from this he passes to a wider vision:

"The German-speaking Jews abroad are a kind of German-speaking province which is well worth cultivation. Nine-tenths of the Jewish world speak German, and a good part of the remainder live in the Islamic world, which is Germany's friend, so that there are grounds for talking of a German protectorate over the whole of Jewry."

By this exploitation of aversions, Dr. Trietsch expects to deposit the Jews of the Pale over Western Asia as "culture-manure" for a German harvest; and if the Jewish migration to Palestine had remained nothing more than a stream of refugees, he might possibly have succeeded in his purpose. But in the last twenty years this Jewish movement has become a positive thing—no longer a flight from the Pale but a remembrance of Zion—and Zionism has already challenged and defeated the policy which Dr. Trietsch represents. "The object of Zionism," it was announced in the *Basle Programme,* drawn up by the first Zionist Congress in 1897, "is to establish for the Jewish people a publicly and legally assured home in Palestine." For the Zionists Jewry is a nation, and to become like other nations it needs its Motherland. In the Jewish colonies in Palestine they see not merely a successful social enterprise but the visible symbol of a body politic. The foundation of a national university in Jerusalem is as ultimate a goal for them as the economic development of the land, and their greatest achievement has been the revival of Hebrew as the living language of the Palestinian Jews. It was this that brought them into conflict with the Germanising tendency. In 1907 a secondary school was successfully started at Jaffa, by the initiative of Jewish teachers in Palestine, with Hebrew as the language of instruction; but in 1914, when a Jewish Polytechnic was founded at Haifa, the German-Jewish *Hilfsverein,* which had taken a leading part, refused to follow this precedent, and insisted on certain subjects being taught in German, not only in the Polytechnic, but in the *Hilfsverein's* other schools. The result was a secession of pupils and teachers. Purely Hebrew schools were opened; the Zionist organisation gave official support; and the Germanising party was compelled to accept a compromise which was in effect a victory for the Hebrew language.

Dr. Trietsch himself accepts this settlement, but does not abandon his idea:

"It was certainly impossible to expect the Spanish and Arabic-speaking Jews[46] to submit in their own Jewish country to the hegemony of the German language.... Only Hebrew could become the common vernacular language of the scattered fragments of Jewry drifting back to Palestine from all the countries of the world. But ... in addition to Hebrew, to which they are more and more inclined, the Jews must have a world-language *(Weltsprache)*, and this can only be German."

Anyone acquainted with the language-ordinances of Central Europe will feel that this suggestion veils a threat. What has been happening in Palestine during the War? Dr. Trietsch informs us that the Ottoman Government has been proceeding with the "naturalisation" of the Palestinian Jews, and that the "local execution of this measure has not been effected without disturbances which are beyond the province of this pamphlet." One significant consequence was the appearance in Egypt of Palestinian refugees, who raised a Zion mule corps there and fought through the Gallipoli campaign. What is the outlook for Palestine after the War? If the

---

46   The Spanish-speaking Jews in Turkey are descended from refugees to whom the Ottoman Government gave shelter in the sixteenth century; the Arabic-speaking Jews have been introduced into Palestine from the Yemen, by the Zionists, since 1908.

Ottoman pretension survives, the menace from Turkish Nationalism[47] and German resentment[48] is grave. But if Turk and German go, there are Zionists who would like to see Palestine a British Protectorate, with the prospect of growing into a British Dominion. Certainly, if the Jewish colonies are to make progress, they must be relieved of keeping their own police, building their own roads, and the other burdens that fall on them under Ottoman government, and this can only be secured by a better public administration. As for the British side of the question, we may consult Dr. Trietsch.

"There are possibilities," he urges, "in a German protectorate over the Jews as well as over Islam. Smaller national units than the 14 1-3 million Jews have been able to do Germany vital injury or service, and, while the Jews have no national state, their dispersion over the whole world, their high standard of culture, and their peculiar abilities lend them a weight that is worth more in the balance than many larger national masses which occupy a compact area of their own."

---

47 Dr. Trietsch admits that Jewish colonisation in Palestine was retarded because "the leading French and British Jews remained under the impression of the Armenian massacres" (of 1895-7) "as presented by the anti-Turkish, French and British Press.... In reality, the butcheries of Armenians in Constantinople were a convincing proof that the Jews in the Ottoman Empire were safe, for ... not a hair on a Jewish head was touched." One wonders how he will exorcise the "Impression" of 1915.

48 As early as 1912 the German Vice-Consul at Jaffa betrayed his annoyance at the progress which Zionism was making. He admits indeed that "the falling off in trade last year would have been greater still than it was, if the economic penetration of Palestine were not reinforced by an idealistic factor in the shape of Zionism;" but he is piqued at the "Jewish national vanity" which makes it advisable for German firms to display their advertisements in Palestine in the Hebrew language and character.

Other Powers than Germany may take these possibilities to heart.

Here, then, are peoples risen from the past to do what the Turks cannot and the Germans will not in Western Asia. There is much to be done—reform of justice, to obtain legal release from the Capitulations; reform in the assessment and collection of the agricultural tithes, which have been denounced for a century by every student of Ottoman administration; agrarian reform, to save peasant proprietorship, which in Syria, at any rate, is seriously in danger; genuine development of economic resources; unsectarian and non-nationalistic advancement of education. But the Jews, Syrians, and Armenians are equal to their task, and, with the aid of the foreign nations on whom they can count, they will certainly accomplish it. The future of Palestine, Syria, and Armenia is thus assured; but there are other countries—once as fertile, prosperous, and populous as they—which have lost not only their wealth but their inhabitants under the Ottoman domination. These countries have not the life left in them to reclaim themselves, and must look abroad for reconstruction.

If you cross the Euphrates by the bridge that carries the Bagdad Railway, you enter a vast landscape of steppes as virgin to the eye as any prairie across the Mississippi. Only the *tells* (mounds) with which it is studded witness to the density of its ancient population—for Northern Mesopotamia was once so populous and full of riches that Rome and the rulers of Iran fought seven centuries for its possession, till the Arabs conquered it from both.

The railway has now reached Nisibin, the Roman frontier fortress heroically defended and ceded in bitterness of heart, and runs past Dara, which the Persians never took. Westward lies Urfa—named Edessa by Alexander's men after their Macedonian city of running waters;[49] later the seat of a Christian Syriac culture whose missionaries were heard in China and Travancore; still famous, under Arab dominion, for its Veronica and 300 churches; and restored for a moment to Christendom as the capital of a Crusader principality, till the Mongols trampled it into oblivion and the Osmanlis made it a name for butchery.

From Urfa to Nisibin there can be fields again. The climate has not changed, and wherever the Bedawi pitches his tents and scratches the ground there is proof of the old fertility. Only anarchy has banished cultivation; for, since the Ottoman pretension was established over the land, it has been the battleground of brigand tribes—Kurds from the hills and Arabs from the desert, skirmishing or herding their flocks, making or breaking alliance, but always robbing any tiller of the land of the fruits of his labour.

"If once," Dr. Rohrbach prophesies, "the peasant population were sure of its life and property, it would joyfully expand, push out into the desert, and bring new land under the plough; in a few years the villages would spring up, not by dozens, but by hundreds."

At present cultivation is confined to the Armenian foothills—an uncertain arc of green from Aleppo to Mosul. But the railway strikes boldly into the deserted middle of the land, giving the arc a chord, and when Turco-German strategic interests no longer debar it from being linked up, through Aleppo, with a Syrian port, it will be the really valuable section of the Bagdad system. The railway is the only capital enterprise that Northern Mesopotamia requires, for there is rain sufficient for the crops without artificial irrigation. Reservoirs of

---

49 Edessa from Thracian [Greek: *bedu*] = Slavonic *voda*.

population are the need. The Kurds who come for winter pasture may be induced to stay—already they have been settling down in the western districts, and have gained a reputation for industry; the Bedawin, more fickle husbandmen, may settle southward along the Euphrates, and in time there will be a surplus of peasantry from Armenia and Syria. These will add field to field, but unless some stronger stream of immigration is led into the land, it will take many generations to recover its ancient prosperity; for in the ninth century A.D. Northern Mesopotamia paid Harun-al-Rashid as great a revenue as Egypt, and its cotton commanded the market of the world.[50]

Southern Mesopotamia—the Irak of the Arabs and Babylonia of the Greeks—lies desolate like the North, but is a contrast to it in every other respect. Its aspect is towards the Persian Gulf, and Rohrbach grudgingly admits[51] that down the Tigris to Basra, and not upstream to Alexandretta, is the natural channel for its trade. It gets nothing from the Mediterranean, neither trade nor rain, and every drop of water for cultivation must be led out of the rivers; but the rivers in their natural state are worse than the drought. Their discharge is extremely variable—about eight times as great in April as in October; they are always silting up their beds and scooping out others; and when there are no men to interfere they leave half the country a desert and make the other half a swamp. Yet the soil, when justly watered, is one of the richest in the world; for Irak is an immense alluvial delta, more than five hundred miles from end to end, which the Tigris and Euphrates have deposited in what was originally the head of the Persian Gulf. The Arabs

---

50 *Muslin* is named after Mosul, and cotton itself (in Greek, Latin, Arabic, and Turkish) *bombyx* or *bambuk,* after Bambyke (Mumbij).
51 "Bagdadbahn," p. 38.

call it the *Sawad* or Black Land, and it is a striking change from the bare ledges of Arabia and Iran which enclose its flanks, and from the Northern steppe-land which it suddenly replaces—at Samarra, if you are descending the Tigris, and on the Euphrates at Hit. The steppe cannot compare with the *Sawad* in fertility, but the *Sawad* does not so readily yield up its wealth. To become something better than a wilderness of dust and slime it needs engineering on the grand scale and a mighty population—immense forces working for immense returns. In a strangely different environment it anticipated our modern rhythm of life by four thousand years, and then went back to desolation five centuries before Industrialism (which may repeople it) began.

The *Sawad* was first reclaimed by men who had already a mastery of metals, a system of writing, and a mature religion—less civilised men would never have attempted the task. These Sumerians, in the fourth millennium B.C., lived on *tells* heaped up above flood-level, each *tell* a city-state with its separate government and gods, for centralisation was the one thing needful to the country which the Sumerians did not achieve. The centralisers were Semites from the Arabian plateau. Sargon of Akkad and Naram Sin ruled the whole *Sawad* as early as 2500 B.C.; Hammurabi, in 1900, already ruled it from Babylon; and the capital has never shifted more than sixty miles since then. Babylon on the Euphrates and Bagdad on the Tigris are the alternative points from which the *Sawad* can be controlled. Just above them the first irrigation canals branch off from the rivers, and between them the rivers approach within thirty-five miles of each other. It is the point of vantage for government and engineering.

Here far-sighted engineers and stronghanded rulers turned the waters of Babylon into waters of life, and the *Sawad* became a great heart of civilisation, breathing in man-power—Sumerians and Amorites and Kassites and Aramaeans and Chaldeans and Persians and Greeks and Arabs—and breathing out the works of man—grain and wool and Babylonish garments, inventions still used in our machine-shops, and emotions still felt in our religion.

"The land," writes Herodotus,[52] who saw it in its prime, "has a little rain, and this nourishes the corn at the root; but the crops are matured and brought to harvest by water from the river—not, as in Egypt, by the river flooding over the fields, but by human labour and *shadufs*[53] For Babylonia, like Egypt, is one network of canals, the largest of which is navigable. It is far the best corn-land of all the countries I know. There is no attempt at arboriculture—figs or vines or olives—but it is such superb corn-land that the average yield is two-hundredfold, and three-hundredfold in the best years. The wheat and barley there are a good four inches broad in the blade, and millet and sesame grow as big as trees—but I will not state the dimensions I have ascertained, because I know that, for anyone who has not visited Babylonia and witnessed these facts about the crops for himself, they would be altogether beyond belief."

Harnessed in the irrigation channels, the Tigris and Euphrates had become as mighty forces of production as the Nile and the Ganges, the Yangtse and the Hoang-Ho.

"This," Herodotus adds,[54] "is the best demonstration I can give of the wealth of the Babylonians: All the lands

---

52 Book I., ch. 193.
53 Cp. Sir William Willcocks. "The Irrigation of Mesopotamia," p. 5 (London, 1911: Spon).
54 Book I., ch. 192.

ruled by the King of Persia are assessed, in addition to their taxes in money, for the maintenance of the King's household and army in kind. Under this assessment the King is maintained for four months out of the twelve by Babylonia, and for the remaining eight by the rest of Asia together, so that in wealth the Assyrian province is equivalent to a third of all Asia."

The "Asia" over which the Achaemenids ruled included Russian Central Asia and Egypt as well as modern Turkey and Persia, and Egypt, under the same assessment, merely maintained the local Persian garrison.[55] Its money contribution was inferior too—700 talents as compared with Assyria's 1,000; and though these figures may not be conclusive, because the Persian "province of Assyria" probably extended over the northern steppes as well as the *Sawad,* it is certain that under the Arab Caliphate, when Irak and Egypt were provinces of one empire for the second time in history, Irak by itself paid 135 million *dirhems* (francs) annually into Harun-al-Rashid's treasury and Egypt no more than 65 million, so that a thousand years ago the productiveness of the *Sawad* was more than double that of the Nile.

Another measure of the land's capacity is the greatness of its cities. Herodotus gives statistics[56] of Babylon in the fifth century B.C.—walls 300 feet high, 75 feet broad, and 58 miles in circuit; three-and four-storied houses laid out in blocks; broad straight streets intersecting one another at regular intervals, at right angles or parallel to the Euphrates. Any one who reads Herodotus' description of Babylon or Ibn Serapion's of Bagdad, and considers that these vast urban masses were merely centres of collection and distribution for

---

55 Herodotus Book III., ch. 91.
56 Book I., chs. 178-183.

the open country, can infer the density of population and intensity of cultivation over the face of the *Sawad*. When the Caliph Omar conquered Irak from the Persians in the middle of the seventh century A.D., and took an inventory of what he had acquired, he found that there were 5,000,000 hectares[57] of land under cultivation, and that the poll-tax was paid by 550,000 householders, which implies a total population, in town and country, of more than 5,000,000 souls, where a bare million and a half maintains itself to-day in city alleys and nomads' tents.

And in Omar's time the *Sawad* was no longer at its best, for, a few years before the Arab conquest, abnormally high floods had burst the dykes; from below Hilla to above Basra the Euphrates broadened into a swamp, and the Tigris deserted its former (and present) bed for the Shatt-el-Hai, leaving the Amara district a desert. The Persian Government, locked in a suicidal struggle with Rome, was powerless to make good the damage, and the shock of the Arab invasion made it irreparable.[58] Under the Abbasid Caliphs of Bagdad the rest of the country preserved its prosperity, but in the thirteenth century Hulaku the Mongol finished the work of the floods, and under Ottoman dominion the *Sawad* has not recovered.

Can it still be reclaimed? Surveys have been taken by Sir William Willcocks, as Adviser to the Ottoman Ministry of Public Works, and his final conclusions and proposals are embodied in a report drawn up at Bagdad in 1911.[59]

---

57 A hectare is approximately equal to two and a half acres.

58 "The Lands of the Eastern Caliphate," by Guy le Strange (Cambridge, 1905: at the University Press), pp. 25-9.

59 "The Irrigation of Mesopotamia," by Sir William Willcocks, K.C.M.G., F.R.G.S. (London, 1911: Spon). The report is dated

"The Tigris-Euphrates delta," he writes, "may be classed as an arid region of some 5,000,000 hectares.... All this land is capable of easy levelling and reclamation. The presence of 15 per cent. lime in the soil renders reclamation very easy compared with similar work in the dense clays of Egypt. One is never far away from the giant banks of old canals and the ruins of ancient towns."

But he does not expect to make all these 5,000,000 hectares productive simultaneously, as they are said to have been when Omar took his inventory. "It is water, not land, which measures production," and he reckons that the average combined discharge of the rivers would irrigate 3,000,000 hectares in winter, and in summer 400,000 of rice or 1,250,000 of other crops. This is the eventual maximum; for immediate reclamation he takes 1,410,000 hectares in hand. His project is practically to restore, with technical improvements, the ancient system of canals and drains, using the Euphrates water to irrigate everything west of the Tigris (down to Kut) and the Shatt-el-Hai, and the water of the Tigris and its tributaries for districts east of that line. Adding 33 per cent. for contingencies to his estimate for cost of materials and rates of labour, and doubling the total to cover interest on loans and subsequent development, he arrives at L29,105,020 (Turkish)[60] as the cost, from first to last, of irrigation and agricultural works together; and he estimates that the 1,410,000 hectares reclaimed by this outlay will produce crops to the value of L9,070,000 (Turkish) a year. In other words, the annual return on the gross expenditure will be more than 31 per cent., and under the present tithe system L7,256,000 (Turkish) of this will remain with

---

Bagdad, March 26th, 1911.

60 60: L1.00 Turkish = approximately L0.90 sterling.

the owners of the soil, while L1,814,000 will pass to the Government. This will give the country itself a net return of 24.9 per cent. on the combined gross cost of irrigation and agricultural works, while the Government, after paying away L443,000 (Turkish) out of its tithes for maintenance charges, will still receive a clear 9 per cent. per annum on the gross cost of irrigation, to which its share in the outlay will be confined.

Unquestionably, therefore, the enterprise is exceedingly profitable to all parties concerned. Looking further ahead, Sir William proposes to supersede the navigation of the Tigris[61] by railways, and so set free the whole discharge of the two rivers for irrigation. He contemplates handling annually 375,000 tons of cereals and 1,250,000 cwt. of cotton, and estimates the future by the effects of the Chenab Canal in Northern India—

"a canal traversing lands similar to those of Mesopotamia in their climate and in the condition in which they found themselves before the canal works were carried out.... In such a land, so like a great part of Mesopotamia, canals have introduced in a few years nearly a million of inhabitants, and the resurrection of the country has been so rapid that its very success was jeopardised by a railway not being able to be made quickly enough to transport the enormous produce."

"A million of inhabitants"—that is the crux of the problem. Labour is as necessary as water for the raising of crops; Sir William's barrages and canals without hands to turn them to account would be a dead loss instead of a profitable investment; but from what reservoir of population is this man-power to be introduced? The German economists are baffled by the difficulty.

---

61   In his immediate project he intends to keep the Tigris navigable, and allots L48,350 (Turkish) for its improvement.

"It is useless," as Rohrbach puts it, "to sink from 150 to 600 million marks in restoring the canal system, and then let the land lie idle, with all its new dams and channels, for lack of cultivators. Yet Turkey can never raise enough settlers for Irak by internal colonisation."[62]

She cannot raise them even for the minor enterprises at Konia and Adapa,[63] and evidently the *Sawad* must draw its future cultivators from somewhere beyond the bounds of Western Asia. From Germany, many Germans have suggested; but German experts curtly dismiss the idea. The first point Rohrbach makes in his book on the Bagdad Railway is that German colonisation in Anatolia is impossible for political reasons. "No worse service," he declares, "can be done to the German cause in the East than the propagation of this idea," and the rise of Turkish Nationalism has proved him right.[64] There remain the Arab lands;

"But even," he continues, "if the Turks thought of foreign colonisation in Syria and Mesopotamia, to hold the Arabs in check" (the political factor again), "that would be little help to us Germans, for only very limited portions of those countries have a climate in which Germans can work on the land or perform any kind of heavy manual labour."

And Germany herself is hard up for men.

"For all prospective developments in Turkey," writes Dr. Trietsch, "not merely scientific knowledge, capital, and organisation are wanted, but men, and Germany has no resources in men worth speaking of for opening up the Islamic world."

---

62 Cp. Wiedenfeld, pp. 62-4.
63 "Die Bagdadbahn," pp. 57, 61.
64 Cp. Wiedenfeld, p. 64.

It is one of his arguments for bringing in the Jews, but the colonisation of Palestine will leave no Jews over for Irak. Rohrbach[65] disposes of the Mouhadjirs—they are a drop in the bucket, and are no more adapted to the climate than the Germans themselves. "There is really nothing for it," he bursts out in despair, "but the introduction of Mohammedans from other countries where the climatic conditions of Irak prevail."

That narrows the field to India and Egypt, and drives Turco-German policy upon the horns of a dilemma:

"The colonists must either remain subjects of a foreign Power, a solution which could not be considered for an instant by any Turkish Government, or else they must become Turkish subjects—"

a condition which, to Indians and Egyptians, as well as Germans, would be prohibitive. No one who has known good government would exchange it for Ottoman government without the Capitulations as a guarantee.

The Ottoman Government has its own characteristic view. In a memorandum on railways and reclamation, published by the Ministry of Public Works in 1909, a *resume* is given of the Willcocks scheme.

"In due time," the memorandum proceeds, "a comprehensive scheme for the whole of Mesopotamia must be carried out, but, apart from the question of expense, it is clear that the public works involved will not be justified until Turkey is in a position to colonise these extensive districts, and this question cannot be considered till we have succeeded in getting rid of the Capitulations."

This is the Ottoman pretension. Egypt, rid of the Osmanli, and India, where he never ruled, have kept

---

65   "Bagdadbahn," p. 83; cp. Trietsch, p. 11.

their ancient wealth of harvests and population, and have man-power to spare for the reclamation of the *Sawad*. All the means are at hand for bringing the land to life—the water, the engineer, the capital, the labour; only the Ottoman pretension stands in the way, and condemns the *Sawad* to lie dead and unharvested so long as it endures.

"The last voyage I made before coming to this country," wrote Sir William Willcocks at Bagdad in 1911, "was up the Nile, from Khartum to the great equatorial lakes. In this most desperate and forbidden region I was filled with pride to think that I belonged to a race whose sons, even in this inhospitable waste of waters, were struggling in the face of a thousand discouragements to introduce new forest trees and new agricultural products and ameliorate in some degree the conditions of life of the naked and miserable inhabitants. How should I have felt if, in traversing the deserts and swamps which to-day represent what was the richest and most famous tract of the world, I had thought that I was a scion of a race in whose hands God had placed, for hundreds of years, the destinies of this great country, and that my countrymen could give no better account of their stewardship than the exhibition of two mighty rivers flowing between deserts to waste themselves in the sea for nine months in the year, and desolating everything in their way for the remaining three? No effort that Turkey can make"—she was then still mistress of the *Sawad*—"can be too great to roll away the reproach of these parched and weary lands, whose cry ascends to heaven."

Turkey, which claims the present in Western Asia, is nothing but an overthrow of the past and an obstruction of the future.

www.ingramcontent.com/pod-product-compliance
Lightning Source LLC
Chambersburg PA
CBHW021212020426
42331CB00003B/319

9 781604 507058